Suck It Up Cupcake, It's Just Withdrawal

Memoirs of The Addiction Fairy

By K. J. Cavalier

SUCK IT UP CUPCAKE, IT'S JUST WITHDRAWAL

INTRODUCTION

"In the beginning God created the heaven and earth," then Adam and Eve just screwed things up for all of us. Trials and tribulations are what our parents use to label all the bad things that we go through in life. Sure, there are bad things that happen to us which leave us asking "why," over and over again. But what about the bad things that we bring on ourselves? Who can we blame for that? So, you made some bad decisions or choices that landed you knee deep in despair, or you chose not to take action, which has led you to have numerous regrets. Life is a learning experience; I mean isn't that what were told, that you can't gain wisdom or learn a valuable lesson until you have experienced things such as let downs, loss or self-destruction. So, does this mean that people who we're born with a silver spoon in their mouth or whatever the saying goes, are idiots and don't know the first thing

Suck It Up Cupcake, It's Just Withdrawal

about street smarts because they have been sheltered from the horrors of the world. I wish I could say the saying "My daddy didn't raise no fool'", but unfortunately I cannot.

Every year the addiction rate goes up, and with it the death rate of overdoses or complications due to excessive use goes up too. I'm not going to bore you with statistics or rant about studies. I truly do not think that someone wakes up one day and says "hey, I'm going to become a drug addict today and completely destroy my life." It's more of chasing a euphoria, a high that makes you feel like all your worries just fade into the darkness that they came from. For the accidental addict who gets stuck on pain meds or anti-anxiety meds to mask a true problem, it's the relief. Sure, we control when to say enough, or do we? What addict has control? I know I didn't. What I had was interdose withdrawal, tolerance withdrawal, and then withdrawal from running out, and withdrawal from quitting. What I had was hell handed to me in a prescription bottle. Anyone who knows withdrawal knows what lengths you'll go through to just feel normal again and stop the madness that you landed yourself in, or possibly a doctor handed you on a piece of paper. Different drugs have different withdrawals; stimulants are different from depressants, then there's

SUCK IT UP CUPCAKE, IT'S JUST WITHDRAWAL

those nice like psychedelics. Some withdrawals are worse than others and some last longer than others. Some can kill you. They all just plain suck. Don't forget about the withdrawal from anti-psychotics and SSRI's, those are drugs too. So, I guess Sally who is truly bi-polar and takes a mood stabilizer which causes withdrawal when she misses a dose, is technically a drug addict too. When we begin an addiction, we surely don't think about withdrawal. Hell, some people didn't even know that withdrawal was a possibility. Desperation is what leads us to do horrible things when we are in withdrawal, this is where most of the rash decisions that take us to rock bottom come from. Things such as stealing or doctor shopping are illegal activities that we would never do when we were not using. Alcoholics always say "I would never steel or break the law to get alcohol." Well when you are taking two shots at 6 am in the morning to ward off the shakes, you are lucky enough to be able to walk to the closest gas station to grab a 6-pack. Alcohol is cheap and easy just like a Las Vegas street walker, so the crime rate with them does tend to be lower, however killing a family in a car accident because you were three sheets to the wind, is pretty much the same thing as robbing a pharmacy, isn't it? No, it's way worse because innocent people die, so you should never believe that one addiction is better than another.

SUCK IT UP CUPCAKE, IT'S JUST WITHDRAWAL

So, I am working on my degree in psychology. My objective is Clinical Psychology with a specialty in addiction and Anger Resolution Therapy. I have a couple years left for my doctorate and am finishing up a few certifications. I'm not going to explain to you the BS of addiction and how it is so bad for you and how you should just say no, because you have probably heard that a million times and it just gets redundant. I am going to explain to you the aftermath of addiction. The stone-cold reality of withdrawal and hitting rock bottom. We're not going to talk about mental illness and how you should seek counseling and work on your behavior and blah blah blah. You should do those things but who wants to read a book about what you should do to better your life when you can just drink a pint of whiskey, and that works just as well, right? I mean why would you want to be the best parent you could be or obtain a degree to be able to hold down an amazing job where you can make lots of money and travel the world when all you should do is trip on some mushrooms and bam, you're seeing the city lights of Amsterdam without leaving your bedroom. Let me just give you a little bit of information and you do with it whatever the hell you want to, or you can even take this book and use your master skills to somehow try and make a bong out of it, so you can smoke all your little problems away, cause your just too sensitive and fragile to deal with

SUCK IT UP CUPCAKE, IT'S JUST WITHDRAWAL

anything anyway. I'm going to explain to you my thought process, and you see if you can relate.

I've been through just about anything you could imagine. Addiction; been through withdrawal from opiates, alcohol, benzos, antipsychotics and antidepressants. Had numerous people die in my arms. I did a stint in prison, actually, it was one night in jail but a stint in prison makes me sound gangster. I've had an abortion. I've been a battered woman and later diagnosed with mental disorders. I've lost everything I own and have been on welfare. Been the victim of date rape, and that will piss you off. I could go on but you get the idea. Grief, embarrassment and total despair was my life for many years. I've had my heart broke and I have even broken a few hearts along the way. I've gone from the worst mother to the absolute best. Most think with a criminal record, their life is ruined along with their reputation. That truly is not the case. I am going to show you how I went from rock bottom to the top. Getting back the respect and gaining more was my favorite part of my recovery. I once in the prime of my addiction, had a man tell me I would never amount to anything, then I spent the next several years after that proving him wrong and continue to today. The only limitations an ex-con or drug

SUCK IT UP CUPCAKE, IT'S JUST WITHDRAWAL

addict has, are the ones that they put on themselves. If you're in the midst of withdrawal, know it will pass, and when it does, that is your second chance in life to start over, to begin again. I never in a million years thought that I would be where I am today. I love more and appreciate everything. It is in our darkest hours, that we gain wisdom, so when the light finally shines, we shine with it. In order to successfully rise from rock bottom, you have to change everything, but especially you have to change your thought process, and it can be done. You will never be the same person you were before; you will be better.

SUCK IT UP CUPCAKE, IT'S JUST WITHDRAWAL

CHAPTER 1-INNOCENCE

Can I say I had a horrible childhood, no! It was actually quite spectacular. I was very sheltered, but was mostly spoiled and babied. My dad worked very hard and my mother did too. My dad drank some beer responsibly and my mother maybe drank twice a year. She smelled weed once and thought it was catnip. I don't recall wanting for anything. I had the overprotective big brother and more friends than a person could ever dream of. My father was one of ten and it seemed as if his side of the family reproduced like rabbits, while my mother was an only child, and guess where I got my spoiledness from. I didn't get to meet my father's parents but heard all the

SUCK IT UP CUPCAKE, IT'S JUST WITHDRAWAL

time how great they were, and my mother's parents were my life. My great grandma Crew lived with grandma and Pap, and passed I believe when I was in the 6th or 7th grade, she was pretty amazing too. Grandma and Pap whereas awesome as they come, but I do remember a few times where my grandmother was going to choke the shit out of Pap, because he fell off the wagon, boy did she keep his ass in check. I truly was given a lot of love and attention and only when my brother got too caught up with his high school girlfriend and ignored me, did I do something bad like run away, into our Jack and Jill bathroom, I shut the doors after I packed food and blankets and just waited it out for change. I was found a couple hours later. I got in trouble.

I was an ass in school. My friends and I were a little on the snooty side and either you liked us or you didn't. We played sports and cheered and acted like our shit didn't stink. We even got into it with each other we were that big of butts. We traded boyfriends, and some of us slept around, while others had long term boyfriends. My friends were partyers but I only drank maybe once in high school and could really just take it or leave it. Towards the end of high school my circle of friends grew and the diversity was really pretty amazing. I hung out with

Suck It Up Cupcake, It's Just Withdrawal

prissiness, jocks, kids that did drugs, kids that wouldn't touch drugs, smart kids, dumb kids, rich kids, poor kids and a few more. I lived in a mobile home park and one of the reasons I loved the high school I went to was that popularity was not based on being wealthy, because a lot of my friends who were popular, lived in the trailer park too. So, I guess you could say I'm straight out da trailer. I tried weed once my senior year, my best friend brought it to me, while I was babysitting. We smoked it out of the back door. I lost two of my closest friends in high school to car accidents and that was horrific, they were actually first cousins and died a few years apart. This I will refer to as life losses #1 And #2.

I'd like to think I lived on the edge. When I turned 16 I took my brothers car to the high school football game with strict instructions not to go anywhere else. I went somewhere else. Myself and five friends took the car to an abandoned house we all thought was haunted. My birthdays on Halloween, no witch jokes please. There were railroad tracks that were probably six feet off the road. I was going 95 mph and only hit the brakes about a foot away from the tracks. Yea, the Dukes of Hazard made it look so fun on TV. Somehow we were not hurt but the

SUCK IT UP CUPCAKE, IT'S JUST WITHDRAWAL

car was totaled. My brother was pissed and his girlfriend of the week thought she could yell at me, no bitch, know your place! I used to fight on occasion too. Well I would beat people up. Run your mouth, get your head pounded into the ground. I think my motto was "don't like em, punch em". This phase of my life might have aided in the future bad karma I was going to go through. No, it was probably the 932 other things I did wrong. I really only got into like five or six fights growing up, but in all honesty, they asked for it, or started it first. The one fight I really enjoyed was with my ex-idiot's side chick. She stalked me so I beat the crap out of her. I should have been grateful she wanted the prick and asked her to take him, but nope, I like losers. At least I used too, finally after 20 years and 4 men, I got it right for the most part.

My first experiment with pain pills was in high school. My grandfather had back problems and I remember seeing a ton of bottles in a drawer in their dining room that were full of big pink pills. The bottle said the words "may cause drowsiness." I cannot even remember what made me take a bottle and take them to school with me. I had never ever had a desire or even knowledge of getting high. If my parents knew this, I would have died by their hands. This was very out of my character but I took a bottle anyway. Maybe I just wanted

SUCK IT UP CUPCAKE, IT'S JUST WITHDRAWAL

to see how being high felt, I really don't know. I slept through a lot of class to the point where my teacher asked my mom if something was wrong with me. She worked at the high school I went to for almost 30 years. My best friend got in my locker and took like ten. She to this day takes and drinks anything she can get her hands on. I had two best friends, I guess you could say a good best friend and a bad one. Obviously, she was the bad one. I got rid of the pills because if she would have overdosed, I would have been in big shit, and she would have been dead. I'm a chicken shit and the reaction I had to them scared me, so I was done with that failed experiment.

My sophomore year in high school I started dating a guy that was four years older than me. It was a ride, his parents hated me because I was very shy around older people, and they interpreted that as me being rude. Looking back, I guess I did have anxiety and fear, but it wouldn't be recognized till many years later. We stayed together with the occasional break up, screw some other guy, get back together. At least I did it when we broke up, he didn't bother with the break up part. I got pregnant like three weeks before graduation but didn't find out until I was about seven or eight weeks along. Boy, was I nauseous. We were married when my beautiful, adorable baby girl was six weeks old. Looking back the wedding was

SUCK IT UP CUPCAKE, IT'S JUST WITHDRAWAL

God awful with peach and green décor. My wedding dress plus my baby fat equaled the Stay Puft Marshmallow Man. We had many friends that spent a lot of time at our house including my lifelong friend Heather, who was married to my cousin Kedrick. We did everything together including trips and sporting events. Heather's parents were my parent's best friends, and we were raised together. Our families did everything together including all of our vacationing, and those truly were the best times of my life. Heather had a huge crush on Kedrick for years, and my father hooked them up. They were married and probably the most adorable couple you would ever come across. We had so many good times together.

So, I got drunk for the first time when I was 20. I know under age, bad person and all that. I was married with a kid. I was home with one of my best friends, the bad one, and we had a little get together like we always had, but they were always responsible gatherings. I think this night my ex and Kevin got toasted and ended up sleeping together in their underwear, in our garden bathtub. Hysterical! My first experience being drunk is, I had three wine coolers. I was outside and a frog came hopping along. I love frogs. They piss on you yes, but I love them. I had to pee. I wanted the frog. I chased the frog as I peed. In my pants. Your first time being drunk is

SUCK IT UP CUPCAKE, IT'S JUST WITHDRAWAL

supposed to be memorable. I'll always remember that. I don't recall feeling bad the next day and that was only one of the very few times you would see me drink throughout the beginning of my adult life. I didn't drink hardly at all and I hated drugs, or I was just too scared to use them. My husband did enough drinking for both of us, or an entire University. I was responsible, for now. I was the DD a lot. We lived in the softball fields. My dad, brother, uncles, cousins, and husband all played together for many years, and there was a lot of drinking. One tournament was even named after a beer. That was my life for many years.

Allen, my husband, was able to get a job that many people desired, at a car manufacturer an hour away. I visited him for lunch and the cat calls from other workers were unreal. I should have known this was bad because there were signs on the doors for divorce attorneys. My already cheater husband was working in a meat market. I was a wonderful mom and wife and started posing for magazines a few months after I was married. I worked at a photography studio and my photographer worked for the local paper, and also shot for magazines. Half-naked chick on a car I was. Hooker! It was a blast though and a real confidence booster. Despite all that, my ex decided it was time to party and come home at 5 am in the morning. You

SUCK IT UP CUPCAKE, IT'S JUST WITHDRAWAL

would think a less than attractive man with a twitch and stutter would be so grateful for my daughter and myself, but no, he had a desire to screw older woman and started on the path of alcoholism, dirty woman, and drugs. He was on the path before that really, it just got out of control at this point. I left him and left everything I had but my daughter. He destroyed my perfect credit and I was back living with my mom and dad, and was just glad to be rid of him once and for all. This is bankruptcy #1. This was also the end of the couple's connection we had with Kedrick and Heather, which I will refer to as loss #3 in life. As you can see I wasn't born into addiction or conditioned by the influence of others. I was and will always be the holder of the key to my own fate. God decides when, and we either accelerate the process or embrace our good health and cherish it.

At this point in life I was fairly still innocent, naive, and felony free. Not even a speeding ticket. I was a good person who followed the law, for the most part, and then began hanging out with police officers, sheriffs and detectives. I don't recall how I got to doing that but I did. At this point, I could still count on one hand how many guys I had slept with. I didn't really appreciate things in life because they really were always just handed to me. I never had to work for anything really, never had to clean

SUCK IT UP CUPCAKE, IT'S JUST WITHDRAWAL

or cook growing up. I think I cleaned my room on occasion but I don't think I was told to. I didn't know how to turn on a vacuum the first time I used one, when I was 27. Shhh, I know that's sad, you don't have to say it under your breath. I loved, but I didn't truly love. I felt good every day and slept great every night. I guess you could say I was untainted. My grandmother, at this time, had suffered mini strokes leading up to a major one, which put her into a vegetable state and that was the first time I truly, deep in my heart, felt pain. My friend's deaths hurt, but this rocked me to my core. This is life loss #4. Eventually my grandmother passed while I was with her by myself, and it was a very unnerving experience I will never forget.

SUCK IT UP CUPCAKE, IT'S JUST WITHDRAWAL

CHAPTER 2-STILL INNOCENT

Vanity was my thing. I was always told I was hot, and it went straight to my head. I went out a lot but usually only on the weekends that my daughter went to her dads. I was hit on constantly. We went to bars in the town of Springfield where I was born, but only lived up until I was two. It was an ok town back then, of course you had your thugs, but nothing like the slum it is today. I think it was ranked like third in a poll of the worse cities to live in. I was always with one friend that was a sheriff, and we had a blast, and obviously with her being in law enforcement, we didn't get into doing bad things. We went out one night with her friends that were also on the force, and as I was sitting at the table with them, a few very handsome guys walked in. All the ladies got a little excited. One was very tall and looked to be built with a beautiful face, another was of average height and build

SUCK IT UP CUPCAKE, IT'S JUST WITHDRAWAL

and had a chiseled, rugged hotness about him. The other
was nothing special so well just act like he wasn't there.
They noticed our table. Somehow later in the evening, my
friend and I were talking to the two attractive ones. I was
talking and dancing with Eric, the rugged hot one, and she
was laughing it up with Aaron, the tall, built and cute one.
Eric and I danced and laughed, and as the night went on,
we gave them a lift to Eric's apartment where Aaron was
staying. We talked awhile, and exchanged numbers, I with
Eric and her with Aaron. Over the next couple of weeks,
we all got to know each other better, and I realized that
Eric was a real ladies man. I was reserved about that, but
at the same time he was so sweet. I really liked him.
Aaron and I talked a lot too on the phone, it was as if we
had become instant friends. Aaron told me that he had
wanted to talk to me first but Eric called dibs, and it
seemed that Eric always got the girl. The boys grew up in
a hick town and were football stars. The funny thing is my
cousins, who I was pretty close with, where friends with
them already. Aaron and I flirted a lot but he was pretty
much seeing my friend as I was seeing Eric. We were all at
the bar that we first met in. I was pretty tipsy, and went
down stairs to the rest room. Aaron was down there and
he was drunk. We were flirting and laughing and five
seconds later, sucking face. We kissed and kissed, and
then my friend walked downstairs and saw us. We went
back upstairs and Eric was pretty upset. The rest is kind of

SUCK IT UP CUPCAKE, IT'S JUST WITHDRAWAL

a blur. That was the beginning of my first real relationship with Aaron, where I actually felt true love, and an orgasm from sex for the first time. Omg, my ex just keeps sucking more and more! I always said the best way to get over a man was with another.

At this point I had just started a pretty decent job that was full time, and with benefits. Keep in mind I had not up to this point, had any desire to go back to school and better myself. It actually didn't even cross my mind. All I ever wanted was to be a wife and mother. Playing house was my career choice. My parents never pushed me to make something of myself. My once perfect credit, where credit card companies would just send me credit cards, was now in shambles and I did not know how to pay bills anymore. My ex smoked, drank and snorted away our money, so I lost all track of being able to pay a bill. It is pretty embarrassing going into a relationship with nothing but a car. Aaron didn't seem to care. He adored me and I him. I had just filed bankruptcy so really didn't have any bills but a car payment, and lived with my parents who didn't make me pay a cent. I was a smoker so I had that expense, plus money to buy clothes to make myself look cute so I could go out looking snazzy. I was still driving the brank new Honda that my ex and I had bought together, and the car payment was pretty cheap because my good credit bought it on a lease. I tire easy of things. I wanted to get rid of the car, so I pretty much had no connection with doofis, but wasn't in the right place in life to go buy a new one. After another year or so I turned it in and did buy an ugly, cheap and crappy car, for which I regret that decision too. Don't worry, eventually I will lose it, so don't feel sorry for me driving a car I don't like just yet.

In the beginning, my relationship with Aaron was made in heaven. Eric, I think, still showed a huge interest in me because I didn't fall all over him, like most girls did. Aaron and I went out one night and when we got home at three in the morning, after we stopped so I could puke from drunkenness, Eric called my mom and dad's house phone. I didn't have a cell phone back in the late 90's, sick I know. He was whining about wanting to be with me while Aaron was sitting next to me. Have you ever wanted to be with two people at the same time, but, know you must make a choice, I have. I chose the lesser of two evils, in reference to stability, trust and a possible future. My parents loved Aaron and he like my previous man, started playing softball with my family, and going on hunting trips. We had land in the southern part of Ohio and had a deer camp every year. Aaron would go with us, and for the first time in my life, I was content and truly happy. My cousins

SUCK IT UP CUPCAKE, IT'S JUST WITHDRAWAL

and uncles loved him as did my brother, so him being taken out in the woods and beaten wasn't a worry I had at the time. Boy when he got drunk though, he was a hoot. "I love your daughter Mike; I love your daughter." We listened to that for an entire evening, but in all honesty, it made me feel good. To know someone adored me.

We were still pretty young at this point, and Aaron sometimes would do a few inconsiderate things, like disappear with a friend when I took the day off to spend with him. This was the first time I noticed that I can be one jealous bitch. He was a little flirtatious with my friends when we would go out, and that was a big no no to me. I got a little tired with things so I dumped him. I miss the days when I could just walk away from a man and not think twice about it. He called me and asked me to come stay with him after this, and I agreed. He said he wanted to talk. I had no idea what he had in mind but I went anyway. When I arrived at his apartment that was almost 30 minutes away, he had a bathtub drawn with candles. We started kissing and then losing pieces of clothing, and were in the bathtub having wet sex by candlelight. In the midst of it, he stopped and proposed to me. Wow, this was my dream. I obviously didn't even think and said "yes." If it looks like a duck and it quacks like a duck, it's

SUCK IT UP CUPCAKE, IT'S JUST WITHDRAWAL

probably a rhinoceros. Isn't that the saying. No, but I often change words and phrases to fit my life. He did not have a ring. Here's your sign. It was an, in the moment proposal. We ended up the next day going to the mall and buying a ring at a jeweler, and I wore that thing like a princess. He is committing, but you're not thinking it out. Let's just run with it and see how it goes. My daughter loving Aaron, was the main issue that was of concern. He was so good with her and I was very lucky, because he understood that she was numero uno. Or did he? At least he acted like it at the time. Some time went by and all was good, until one day while we were at a friend's, I got the impression that Aaron wasn't as happy and ready to get married as I was, when he was asked about our plans for the wedding.

I often on the weekends when Kendal was at her dad's, went to Aarons to stay until she came back on Sunday evening. One weekend he seemed a little distant. He out of nowhere said he was going out that night with friends. Hello, I am at your house for the weekend. We fought a little. Then we fought a lot. I took off my ring and handed it to him and said I was done. He agreed and said he did not want to get married, or even be together. I was broken beyond reality. I felt a pain deep in my core, and didn't even know how to grasp what had just

SUCK IT UP CUPCAKE, IT'S JUST WITHDRAWAL

happened. I did the fake I'm ok crap, and acted like I was fine with it. All the while, inside, I felt as if I was going to lose my mind. I left and was beyond devastated. I tried to function normally, and all the time, he and I for some reason, are still talking here and there. I chased, I won't lie. I was not accepting that it was over. Never chase a person if they don't want to be with you. I know it hurts, but it just makes matters worse. We saw each other a few times, and then one day he asked me to go to a wedding with him. I agreed. Like I'm going to say no. We went and where drinking a bit. We had a tent, and slept outside under the beautiful July stars. Eric was there, as was a lot of Aaron's other friends. We went upstairs in the house so I could change my clothes in the bathroom. We started kissing and ended up having sex on the bathroom floor. In the middle of getting it on, he again stopped and said I want to have a baby. What the hell is wrong with this guy. I didn't stop him because again, the whole playing house thing, and at the time I thought he was the love of my life. We got back together but things seemed to be a little different, like we weren't close friends and lovers anymore. A little while later I went to his apartment for the weekend and he again dropped a bomb on me. In all this time, we were not using protection, but I was not getting pregnant. He told me he was seeing someone else, and that he had gotten close with her brother, and they have done things together. She was a chiropractor and

SUCK IT UP CUPCAKE, IT'S JUST WITHDRAWAL

that was what Aaron was all about, monetary gain. This was the first nail in my coffin and what I will refer to as life loss #5. At this time, I received a phone call while I was at work. My dad had been dealing with some health concerns, so he had gone to the doctor a week before. The call was my mother stating that my father was just diagnosed with Chronic Lymphocytic Leukemia. My father had terminal cancer, and this begins my life of depression, mental illness, addiction and despair.

SUCK IT UP CUPCAKE, IT'S JUST WITHDRAWAL

CHAPTER 3-I'LL TAKE A TICKET TO THE LOONEY BIN PLEASE, JAIL WILL WORK TOO

While Aaron and I were coming to the end of our three-year relationship, I had my second laparoscopy for endometriosis. I had to take pain pills after the operation, but stopped once the pain from the surgery was gone. When I found out my father was pretty much going to die, I developed the most severe neck pain you could ever imagine. It was interfering with my daily functioning in life. I now know that this was stress and depression that decided to take root in the form of neck pain. I went to my family doctor who prescribed me 100 tramadol with three refills, and a muscle relaxer to boot. I was taking them as prescribed and just kept getting skinnier and skinnier, due to the onset of a horrific depression. I was at this point, just going through the motions of life. I would call Aaron and he pretty much would blow me off like I had never been anything to him, so I was forced to accept the fact that we were over. I was very close with my father and relied on him for everything. I was close with my mother too, but I idolized my father and just wanted to follow him everywhere he went. The obsession he had with my daughter, and she with him, was real. That was his girl. I was lucky to have him, as he was my support in life. At this point I started going out a lot more and dating numerous guys, to try and get over Aaron. I was taking pills and would go on the weekends and drink a little, but it was in no way an addiction at this point. It was the beginning of one.

I was a shell of my former self. I was a mom, but I wasn't a mom. I had never had to cope with such despair in my life and realize now that I pretty much didn't have one useful coping skill. I started getting more pain pills because I was doubling up. They made my neck stop hurting, and I had less cares while taking them. They gave me a high that I really liked, but when they wore off, I needed to take more to feel the same effect. This cycle went on for several months, and then I started going to the hospital for a fake tooth ache being given hydrocodone and an antibiotic. I didn't bother getting the antibiotic filled because well, my fellow opiate addicts understand. At this point it's still not addiction, it's downright abuse. I went to a dentist and got a prescription for hydrocodone again. This time I thought I would stick it in the copy machine and make a copy to get filled, to have more. I had no idea that I was committing a crime. I did not have any knowledge of laws, in reference to drugs, because they had never been an issue in my life, nor had anyone I known been arrested. I took it to a pharmacy and they filled it. I did it again, taking it to a national grocery store pharmacy and this time they said it would be a little while, and had me wait, so I waited. After about 25 minutes a police officer walked to the pharmacy window, then went into the back with the pharmacist. She came out and the police officer accused me of presenting a false prescription. I was in awe because like I said, my dumb ass didn't know I was breaking the law. Sure, I knew it probably wasn't right, but not to the extent that I was now placed in hand cuffs and my purse was being searched. I had purchased pink and green containers to put all of my antidepressants in, two different ones, because my family doctor had also given me samples of those. I don't think she was buying what I was selling and automatically labeled me a drug addict. She stood me up and lead me out of the store while reading me my rights. I made a fool of myself crying I have never been arrested before, and that I hadn't even had a speeding ticket. She placed me in the back of the cruiser and whisked me to jail.

The humiliation of being arrested is real. I was taken into the deep dark pits of the basement of the

SUCK IT UP CUPCAKE, IT'S JUST WITHDRAWAL

county jail where actual criminals were. I was put in a cold and dreary cell with just a concrete slab to lay on and a toilet and sink. At this point I am shaking in my shoes and have no idea what is about to go down, but I'm pretty sure it's me. I was taken into a small room where they took my picture and finger printed me. The lady tried to talk to me like I was sane and not facing my first stint in the slammer. I couldn't even function at this point. When she was done, I was escorted back to my holding cell and just waited, and waited some more. Then I waited. That went on for hours. They let me out to make a call. No one was home at my house and I just couldn't get ahold of anyone. They then put me back in my cell to wait. I waited. Then I waited some more. They came to get me to strip me of my clothes and dignity, and made me take a shower right after they stuck their fingers in my ass and coola. This is hideous. I got dressed in a very fashionable and high end orange jump suit that read "jail" across the back, and then was taken up to the actual cells with the other female inmates. I don't care how tuff I used to be and how many chicks I had beat up, at this point I was the biggest pussy curled up into the fetal position, just waiting to get shanked. I thought it was the end. Everyone talked to me and seemed pretty nice. I kept thinking to myself that I was too good to be in here with these criminals, completely dismissing the idea that I was a bleeping

SUCK IT UP CUPCAKE, IT'S JUST WITHDRAWAL

criminal now. I relaxed a bit and made a collect call, to my sister-in-law, aint no way I'm calling my daddy. The call announced "you have a collect call from a County Jail Inmate, do you accept the call?" All I heard was "do what?" In an almost screaming fashion. Somewhere in that announcement I had to say my name so she knew sure as shit, it was me. She had to break the news to the family. My mom said my father cried. That made my depression worse. My dad found an attorney and the next day at arraignment, they let me out on my own recognizes. My mom and dad were crushed. At this point I stopped the pills, for a minute.

One of my other good friends that was a detective for the same police force, that just threw me in the slammer, stayed by my side through this. It was the day of my pre-trial and he showed up to show his support, because he knew I was scared and this was not something I had been through before. He took his detective badge off and put it in his pocket then stated that the judge sometimes doesn't care for cops because his wife had an affair with one. Great Mike, why don't you just go ahead and convict me yourself. As I stood before the judge I shook. My parents looked on in utter terror. My attorney spoke and said the same damn thing I had been trying to tell them, that I had never been arrested and so on. People who have criminal records have to start somewhere, they all had their first arrest too. But I was better than them. The judge ordered pre-trial probation and the case would be dismissed if I attended a rehab, and six months of probation. I walked out with a little relief but rehab really, that is for drug addicts. I am no drug addict. With my probation, I literally just had to mail a card in once a month. I went for an assessment at a public rehab facility in the County where I lived, and they put me in a beginners group that met one night a week. Rehab for beginners, that's another book in itself. I went to my first meeting, and the lead of the group asked everyone why they were there. He got to me and I made up some bullshit, and then he accused me of being a criminal. I am no criminal sir. Illegal activity, handcuffs, joy ride in a cop cruiser, night in jail, mind raped by Lucy the B&E bandit, and standing in front of a judge with an attorney, but still not a criminal. I do believe this is the point that delusional and ignorant are terms I used to refer to myself. Lucky me at this point, had a real-life toothache. Karma I know. Went to the dentist for him to give me what, hydrocodone and antibiotics. So, the next week when I was drug tested, I tested positive. The only thing that saved me was the fact that my face was the size of Utah from the swelling, and my dentist called my counselor to tell them that I had a nasty abscess. I was on probation, and this was a

SUCK IT UP CUPCAKE, IT'S JUST WITHDRAWAL

probation violation. Still, I didn't grasp the severity, and I pretty much got out of it without a scuff, but a lot of embarrassment. Good news, my name made it into the newspaper, bad news, it was the criminal section. This was life loss #5, my reputation.

I was stupid enough to go out and drink while I was on probation. At this point I am not making any good decisions and am in a deep dark place mentally. I went out a lot with my cousins and their friends, funny thing is, these are the same friends that hung out with my ex-husband and I had made comments about how bad they were, and how my husband shouldn't be around them, just a few years earlier. I had no idea that Cory, my younger cousins best friend, was desperately in love with me. We went to Cory and another friend's house that was some ways away after a long day of drinking at the ball field and then at the bar. Brian, which was another one of my cousin's friends, did a lot of drugs. I ended up passing out in Cory's bed early because I had just drunk way too much. Everyone else stayed up and partied. I woke the next morning to complete devastation. I was wearing just a t-shirt and Brian was lying next to me in bed. I can't recall why I wasn't livid but I was very uncomfortable and mad at my cousin for allowing him to come into the room with me. Felt this was my fault for it happening, because

SUCK IT UP CUPCAKE, IT'S JUST WITHDRAWAL

the state I was in when I went to bed, not to mention I had no memory of what we had done at all. A few weeks went by and I was starting to get very sick. I ended up going to Urgent Care and was given a urinalysis. I was really wanting more pills and something for nausea but the nurse came in and told me I was pregnant. I was in shock. I cried and wanted to just kill Brian, but the only thing that kept crossing my mind was how many birth defects this child would have because of the drugs and alcohol that both of us used. I knew I had to get an abortion. Miranda, which was my cousin's girlfriend, which was my friend that I introduced to my cousin, called Brian and told him he needed to pay half of the abortion. He agreed. When Miranda and I arrived at the clinic, it was like an abortion mill. Girls were lined up to terminate a mistake they had made. I went through with it and it was pretty painless, some minor cramping and they had advised me I was five weeks along. I laid around all day after Miranda dropped me off at my mom and dad's house. A couple weeks later Miranda and I had gotten into a fight and the first thing she did was take the consent form for the abortion and give it to my brother. My brother is very different. An ok guy one minute, and your worst enemy the next. The first thing he did was take it to my dad. He constantly tried to make my father hate me because he thought my parents babied me too much. My parents were devastated and my father after confronting me, and me denying it, walked away with tears in his eyes. This baby, who I cry for often these days, was life loss #6.

    I finished probation and treatment successfully and went on about my merry way. I was going out a lot at this point, when I should have been staying at home trying to better myself from the stupid crap I had pulled, but my dad was still dying and I was still heartbroken. I went out one night with friends and noticed a handsome man that was tall and of average build. There was just something about him that caught my eye. He was very professional and different than any of the guys you would typically see hanging at the bars we went to. He noticed me too. He found a reason to talk to me in a subtle flirtatious way, at the latter part of the night, and I found myself a little shy. I was intimidated I guess. I left and never thought about it again. Another friend of mine and myself went out a couple weekends later and sure enough, he was there. My brother met up with us and as Adam, my new interest, and I were talking, my brother approached us. Adam put out his hand to shake my brothers as he introduced himself with a polite "nice to meet you". This was different than what I was used to and Adam and I spent the rest of the evening talking. At this point I was plastered and I left the bar with Adam and his friend. I didn't even know this guy really. We went to Steak and Shake and as we sat, I

SUCK IT UP CUPCAKE, IT'S JUST WITHDRAWAL

nodded off on Adams arm. I passed out. He took care of me and even took me to the bathroom. After that we went back to his apartment and had drunk sex. The kind of sex where your there, but you're not there. Adam lived above a cell phone store that he had owned. And over the next few weeks, I started spending a lot of time there.

One of the busy bodies I worked with, overheard the scanner of my arrest so work knew about it before I had the chance to tell them. We had monthly audits at my job, that I had been at for three years now, and on my audit, that followed my arrest, I apparently lied about the production I had done for a day, and was fired. Time to look for a new job. That was fun seeing how I had just caught myself a criminal record. I looked around for a while and found a position with a telemarketing company, because that was about all I could find. Something seemed strange with the company. It was a little backwoods, with two guys that ran it, being a little creepy. I went in one morning to one of the owners snorting an oxy on the counter. He asked me if I wanted one. "Hell no I'm not sticking anything up my nose except my finger," I told him. He proceeded to ask me if I would get bounded to the company, and I advised him that I had a record, so he then asked another girl. Luckily she said no. At this point I had brought one of my friends in to work with us,

SUCK IT UP CUPCAKE, IT'S JUST WITHDRAWAL

and we had just talked the day before about how we thought something was fishy. Later in the same day, I received a phone call from an older lady. She advised me that the two owners of the telemarketing company I was working for, were painting her house, and that she had paid them but they did not come and do the work. She also advised me that her check book was missing. I started snooping around on the computer and noticed there were no records of any of the donations that were given to the company. The company's objective was to raise money for a charity. Everything just seemed wrong. My friend and myself, along with the girl that worked with us, went to see my friends at the police station. A detective for that type of crime sat down with us and took our statements. When he escorted us out, I dropped my cell phone. I blurted out "oh crap," and Julie, my friend, just laughed and told me not to worry about it, because my new boyfriend owned Digital Connection, and he would just get me a new one. The detective turned around and glared at me fiercely and said, "you're not dating Adam Michaels are you?" I responded that I indeed was, and he proceeded to tell me to stay far away from him. I was a little shocked and asked why. He told me he could not tell me, but that he had been under investigation for 12 years with the police department. I pretty much dismissed what he had said and we left. A couple days later we received a phone call from the local newspaper to do an anonymous

SUCK IT UP CUPCAKE, IT'S JUST WITHDRAWAL

interview about the telemarketing company, and then a few days after that, it was all over the television that the police raided the office and a man hunt entailed. They finally found them a few states down south, and charged them each with several criminal counts, ranging from fraud to theft. I was very relieved about this but now had doubts and fears about this mysterious handsome man I was dating, that I truly knew nothing about, but that my friends, is another chapter, literally.

SUCK IT UP CUPCAKE, IT'S JUST WITHDRAWAL

CHAPTER 4-IT'S ALL DOWNHILL FROM HERE

Adam and I had been in a relationship at this point for about a week. I was spending time at his apartment and left a few of my belongings. I had already got the impression that he hung out in bars a lot. I did, but it was a weekend thing as his, I believe was more of a weekend and weekday thing. A bar was in walking distance from his apartment and he took advantage of that. I called him all evening because I needed to get my curling iron and makeup that I had left at his house. He was not responding and I knew he was at the bar. I have very jealous tendencies and this pissed me off. I drove to his apartment and he wasn't home, so I walked to the bar

SUCK IT UP CUPCAKE, IT'S JUST WITHDRAWAL

to see if he was there. Low and behold I walk in, and he is sitting at the bar, pretty close to a blonde in a barstool next to him. He turned and saw me and said "hey you, would you like a drink?" I said no and told him I needed my stuff and he needed to come let me get it. I was livid. He acted a little mad and we walked back to his apartment. We had a few words and he yelled at me and called me a bitch. Again, here is your sign to abort mission. I left and his drunk rear walked back to the bar. I was done. The next day I did not call him and he didn't call me. Then, the day after that, my phone rang. It was him apologizing asking me if I wanted to go to his parents' house at Lake Erie. I caved and agreed to go. I was off and on pills at this point, but was not feeling any type of withdrawal when I did not use them. He picked me up. My daughter was at her dad's for the weekend, and we drove almost three hours to get there. It was nice meeting his family, although that is one of my biggest hates in life, because I am pretty much intimidated by everything in life, especially meeting parents. Adams mother was very polite and personable, while his dad didn't speak much but was still nice when I met him. We went out on their boat and enjoyed the rest of the weekend.

My abuse at this point is getting deeper and very soon will turn into an addiction. I was using pills more on a daily basis and anyone who has been addicted to a drug, knows that daily use is what sets us up for dependence and withdrawal. Adam and I had been dating a while, and I was able to hide my addiction from him. I was ready to make things more permanent with us, so I decided that a baby would do that. He thought that I was on birth control but that would be a responsible decision, and I just didn't do things like that. A few months into the relationship, I had a feeling in my gut, literally, so I took a pregnancy test and sure enough I was pregnant. I went to his car dealership, that he owned, and showed him the test. I think he was in awe at first, but then it kind of sank in. He smiled a scared, excited smile, and we went on. I was about four months pregnant, and it is amazing how a doctor would give you pain pills, and not even have any idea that you were pregnant. I still used during my pregnancy and thought that was OK, because pain pills can be used at that time, not knowing about withdrawal, or the harm it would do to the baby. I was pretty deep at this point. Adam and I went to visit his parents in their hometown, that he was born in. It was in the Cleveland area. I had run out of pills the morning we had left for the three-hour drive, and didn't think anything of it. By that night I was feeling horrible. It was a chemically induced type of anxiety I had never felt before. My nerves were on fire and I was very jittery and on edge. I didn't sleep at all

SUCK IT UP CUPCAKE, IT'S JUST WITHDRAWAL

that night, and the next day woke up feeling even worse. We went to his grandparents' house for dinner, where his grandmother was suffering from terminal cancer. She was so fragile, but was such a sweet woman. His grandparents were in their late seventies and time had taken their toll on them. I was feeling just horrible. I went into the bathroom and searched the medicine cabinet to see if there may be some kind of pain pills that I could take to get me by. Nothing. We were sitting at the dinner table when I looked up to see medicine bottles on the buffet. My wheels where turning, trying to figure out how I could read them, and take a few if they were pain pills. Everyone went into the living room to talk as I got up to go to the bathroom, again and again. Finally, I just grabbed a huge bottle that I was able to see that it said they may cause drowsiness. I didn't even check to see what they were. I am pregnant and didn't even have the thought in my mind that these may hurt my unborn child. I took them to the bathroom with me, and took a couple, then placed the bottle into my coat pocket. In just a few minutes I started to feel better. We left and I was elated that I had just gotten away with what I had done, and again didn't think, because I had just taken a dying cancer patients pain medicine, and she was going to be left with nothing to take. This didn't cross my mind until years later. We went back home and resumed things as usual. Going to the lake and Adam's parents' house

SUCK IT UP CUPCAKE, IT'S JUST WITHDRAWAL

was something that we did often, usually every weekend. At this point Adam is getting close with Kendal, and we are starting to look like we are going to be a family. Adam came one day to pick me up and said he had a surprise for me. We drove into Springfield into a nice neighborhood, and he showed me a house. He was smiling and went on to tell me that he had just rented this house for us to move into. I was ecstatic with joy and thought this is it, we are going to be a family. The house was huge and beautiful, and we started on the process of moving in. We received a call that Adam's grandmother had passed so we made plans for the trip for the funeral. We went to his grandfathers after the funeral, for the wake, and again I had run out of pills. I did the unthinkable once more, and took a bottle of pills off of the buffet that belonged to his grandfather, and then proceeded to put the entire bottle deep down into the lining of a leather coat that I was wearing. Again, we left and I had thought I had gotten away with it.

The house was decorated and really seemed like a home. One evening when we were just sitting watching TV, there was a knock at the door. It was Adam's mom, sister, and my father. My dad had a look of fierce anger on his face, and everyone came in. We sat on the

SUCK IT UP CUPCAKE, IT'S JUST WITHDRAWAL

couch and my father stood on the stairs that led to the living room. Adam's mom advised us that his grandparent's pills were missing, and she asked us if we had taken them. They said the first time, when it was his grandmother's pills, they had thought that maybe in her old age, she had just misplaced them, but when his grandfathers had disappeared, they knew someone had taken them. His mother told me that she loved me, and that if I needed help that they would help me. Adam held my hand and had tears rolling down his face. I denied it to the end, even though it was blatantly obvious, that it was me. I had never been confronted about something like that, and when I am scared, I cry. My father knew it was me because of my previous arrest, but Adam and his family had no idea. I tried to keep it that way. They left, and we went to bed like usual. No longer was it abuse, but at this point it was addiction in the worst way. I doctor shopped and visited hospitals to feed my addiction, but was getting further along and thought it was time to start using the phone to call doctors during emergency hours. I called previous dentists to complain of an abscess. I called doctors that I had never been to before, and pretended to be a patient. I was starting to become a first-rate criminal. All the while this is going on, things with Adam seemed to be even more mysterious than when we first got

SUCK IT UP CUPCAKE, IT'S JUST WITHDRAWAL

together. People were showing up at our door in the middle of the night, looking for him, demanding money, and when I asked about it, I was given no answer. I would stop at the car lot, only to find Adam talking with a group of guys, who rapidly dispersed when I drove up. He's not giving me answers to anything, but I really didn't care about things at that point. As long as I had some pills, I was good, nothing else really mattered. I used to be such a good mother, and now I had begun, in a way, neglecting my daughter mentally, but I still took care of her because I knew I had to, it was my duty. My dad is getting sicker, and so am I.

        Adam was supportive and went to the baby doctor visits and ultrasound. I was huge and gained so much weight developing high blood pressure. I was at least smart enough in my eighth month of pregnancy, to go off the pills so that the baby didn't feel horrible when it was born. I was very sick for a few days, but was early in the addiction, for it not to be too horrendous. This probably had a lot to do with the high blood pressure. While I was on pills, my blood pressure was fine, probably because they relaxed me and the stress of life didn't bother me. We found out it was a boy and decorated the nursery in preparation. I was scheduled to be induced and

SUCK IT UP CUPCAKE, IT'S JUST WITHDRAWAL

went into the hospital on a Monday morning. They started the Pitocin. Within two hours the labor had hit me hard but I was only dilated to a two. It was time for the epidural and as they sat me up, performed the procedure, and laid me back down, I felt as if I needed to push. She checked me and sure enough I was now at a ten. The baby flew out, literally, and the doctor caught him in midair. This ripped my vaginal area to pieces but that made me happy because that would mean that I could get pain pills, and get them easily. I gave birth to a dark-haired baby boy, that weighed six pounds and seven ounces and I named him Adam Anthony Michaels Jr., his dad picked his name obviously. We took him home and I resumed my addiction as if I had never left off. I found a job, and Adam had found a babysitter for Adam Jr., after about two months. I had only been on the job about three months and was missing so much work, because of needing pills so I forged a doctor's excuse, and gave it to our Human Resources manager. It was actually a letter, on police letterhead, that said I was helping in an investigation and needed to meet with detectives on a regular basis. The things you will do during an addiction are unbelievable, but that was where I was. I managed to get arrested again for forgery but the prosecutor thought it was so petty, and I had already lost my job for it, so he just dismissed the charges. I lucked out again with a slap on the wrist. Adam, I think, at this point is truly beginning to tire, but I

SUCK IT UP CUPCAKE, IT'S JUST WITHDRAWAL

didn't care, as long as I had my pills. He truly loved me, and I was the mother of his child, so he stuck it out and hoped for the best, at least I thought that at the time.

My tolerance has risen because I am fairly into the addiction now. Four hydrocodone or six tramadol at a time, three to four times a day is the norm. Once the high wears off, I will begin to get a little shaky and feel as if I have the flu. In order to stop this from happening, I start dosing sooner. Adam still owned the cell phone store and we were invited to Las Vegas for a convention with other cell phone dealers for Sprint. It was Nextel and then bought by Sprint and that is what the convention was introducing to the dealers. We were getting ready to leave but I did not have that many pain pills, so I went to the dentist and obtained a prescription. I needed a lot of pills because it was a three-day trip, so I made about ten copies, and took it to about ten different pharmacies in my town and a town next to it. It was only a prescription for ten pills, so all in all, I had about fifty to hold me over as some pharmacies would not fill it. It was apparent it was a copy, and while they advised me they couldn't fill it; they didn't go into detail, or explain anything about that to me. I had an emergency script I had planned to get filled in

SUCK IT UP CUPCAKE, IT'S JUST WITHDRAWAL

Vegas when we got there. We flew out and had a great time on Friday night, with going to the convention the next evening. I walked to a pharmacy right by the hotel to get my script filled, but they would not fill it, and when I asked why, they said it was out of state and that the doctor would have to call it in. I just tried to tuff it out because somehow I was already out. We went to the convention and I was feeling very ill, I was in withdrawal. My head aches, noises were so loud and my whole body hurt. Sprint supplied an open bar after the convention and Adam took full advantage of it. I was too sick to drink. We went to the room and Adam laid down to go to bed. I told him I was going to go gamble or go to the pool and I grabbed a back pack and headed out. I walked the strip and asked where the nearest hospital was. I needed pills or I wouldn't make it the next day. I walked five miles in downtown Las Vegas, past hookers, through dark scary alleys, until I arrived at the hospital. I complained of a tooth ache and was given a prescription for my life line, hydrocodone. I walked five miles back to a pharmacy and got the prescription filled. When I arrived back at the room, hours later, Adam had the police looking for me. I am a really good liar at this point, and told him I met an older lady at the pool and we hung out for a while. We finished up the weekend with a Nascar race and the next day, got on the plane to fly home. I had run out of pills again so the flight home was hideous. Every

SUCK IT UP CUPCAKE, IT'S JUST WITHDRAWAL

time we go out of town, Adam was having to take me to a hospital, because I either had a tooth ache or a migraine, or my favorite, the cramps. I can't tell you how many vaginal exams I had for phantom pain. That got old fast, and to this day I will only go to the gynecologist once every five years.

I started working at the cell phone store now, and was just stealing Adam blind. Writing bad checks and just about anything to fuel my addiction. Adams office was in an adjoining part of the building and there was a lock on the door. I somehow got the door open and searched for checks I could use to pay for pills, because I am spending on the average about $120.00 every two days. Adam went into a psychotic state when he realized I got into his office. The addiction has consumed me. I took Adam Jr. to work with me every day, and was completely exhausted between the pills, not eating, and being a mom. I do not recall what got me started on buying the tramadol over the internet. It was like I had struck the lottery, no doctors or pharmacies, just order and pay COD. This was expensive, so I was now doing things that were just down right stupid. Spending peoples deposits they put down on phones, you name it. Adam was in a downward spiral as well. He couldn't make payroll every week. Our utilities

SUCK IT UP CUPCAKE, IT'S JUST WITHDRAWAL

were always getting shut off. People would come looking for him all the time. My son and I would go to work and there wouldn't be heat, and Adam would just leave us there all day without food or running water. The place began to smell from the trash and toilet not being flushed. One of Adam's acquaintances stopped in the store and we were just sitting there talking. He was pretty upset that the baby and I had been left in this mess. He proceeded to tell me somethings that kind of verified my suspicions, that Adam was not on the up and up. I didn't have pills and it was not time for any of my refills, so I called a doctor in another town that I had never been to before, to call in a prescription. He called it in, and when I went to get it, I had a medical card and it was free pills. They only had part of the prescription and advised me the rest would be in the next day. I called the next day to ask when it would be ready and they wanted to know what time I would be there to get it. I gave them a time, and then my son and I went to pick them up. As I was walking out, a detective stopped me, asked my name, then asked me to follow her. "Oh shit!" She told me that there were five felony warrants out for me, and I needed to call someone to get Adam Jr. because I was going to jail. My father, heartbroken again, came to get him, and I went to jail for the third time. This time its felonies, and this time its serious shit. Detectives from the adjoining county also were looking for me. Turns out the false prescription

SUCK IT UP CUPCAKE, IT'S JUST WITHDRAWAL

spree I went on before Vegas, caught up with me. I was given two years' probation in two counties, and decided to get clean. Before I did, I overdoses in the car because Adam had done an intervention with my parents. I didn't want to die; I was reaching out for help. I wanted a stay in the psych ward to detox me. I was taken to the ER where they poured charcoal down my throat, then proceeded to pump my stomach. You would have thought that that was a lesson but it wasn't. Adam had become mean and things were starting to get a little violent. He controlled my every move, and when I didn't follow his direction, he would repossess my car, which I got from his Buy Here Pay Here car lot. We were forced to move from our house into one of his rundown slum apartments, and the day we moved, he was in a rage. He screamed and threw things at me the entire day. I was outside packing my car when Kendal came out and said he had grabbed her arm, and threw her to the ground. I went in livid and got in his face. He picked me up over the stairs and slammed my head into the doorframe. He then took my cell phone from me. Kendal ran next door to call the police. Adam was taken to jail for domestic violence. I later had the charges dismissed and we got back together. So, begins a real, hard, nightmare of withdrawal. This is life loss #8, my freedom and clean record, all charges before this were dismissed.

SUCK IT UP CUPCAKE, IT'S JUST WITHDRAWAL

Acute withdrawal from opiates lasts about five days, and I had just done a cold turkey again. With each start and stop of narcotics, you will have kindling, where each withdrawal gets worse and worse. At the point that I had just stopped, I was also taking around ten tramadol, four times a day, so this made it even more grueling. You feel like you have the most horrifying case of the flu, on top of chemically induced anxiety. Now I'm not talking about anxiety that you get because you were scared or you're in a nervous situation, chemically induced anxiety is all of your nerves feeling as if they are on fire at the same time. Your head pounds, you sweat, and the nausea is just debilitating. Insomnia is a whole different story. Sleeping pills didn't even help. It was agony 24/7 for five days. Sound shook me to my very core and let's not talk about bright lights. On the sixth day, I was feeling a little better but still very edgy and had minor flu like symptoms. This went on for a few days, and then I went into a full state of being wired. I have never taken acid or tried coke, but I'm pretty sure snorting 32 lines all at once, is what I felt like. Despite the sorrow I was still feeling for my dad, and just life in general, I hit my pink cloud. You love life in the pink cloud. You feel good after being so ill for a while, and you feel like you can take on the world. I was so loud, because I was so wired, and it was almost as if I had regressed into adolescence. I was acting very immature and even started dressing like a teen. I still had insomnia but felt like a

SUCK IT UP CUPCAKE, IT'S JUST WITHDRAWAL

million dollars. With my emotions being numbed for so long, I didn't realize that I had grown, to completely detest Adam. In fact, I didn't want to be with him, and it was obvious, but I stayed with him for Adam Jr., and for Kendal, to have a family, so all the wrong reasons. I went to see the psychiatrist at mental health and Adam went with me. He told the doctor that I was being very mean and showing a lot of anger. Of course I was dumbass, you control my every move and I am completely dependent upon you while you take advantage of that, is what I was thinking. The doctor put me on an anti-psychotic medication, she called it a mood stabilizer. I had never even heard of anything like that before, but at this point in my life, I didn't think too much about what I put into my body. I started taking it, and slowly started detaching myself from Adam.

SUCK IT UP CUPCAKE, IT'S JUST WITHDRAWAL

CHAPTER 5-AM I A STAR IN A MOVIE?

I left Adam and moved in with my brother. He was recently divorced because his wife cheated on him and he seriously had, and still has, issues with being alone. We would go out and Adam would call to complain, even calling my father to call me and get me to go home. This was making me mad because my dad was sick and all he would do was call and get him involved, when I was trying to move away from him observing all the bad in my life. My brother was always a lady's man, and all of my friends had huge crushes on him, including Lisa, my bad best

SUCK IT UP CUPCAKE, IT'S JUST WITHDRAWAL

friend. Somehow Lisa and Colton, my brother, where
talking on the phone a lot. I didn't have a vehicle because
Adam again repossessed it when I left him, so I was driving
my brother's truck a lot. He had me go to Columbus to
pick Lisa up and bring her back to his house so we could all
go out. At this point I'm doing great and getting away
from Adam, is part of my recovery, as I was previously
advised in rehab by my counselor. She told me that I
would never get better unless I got away from Adam. Lisa
was so annoying and was a very pushy person that would
do anything to get her way. Usually everything out of her
mouth was a lie and she was very manipulative. We were
getting ready to go out and I put my brother's belt on. She
cried for over an hour that she wanted the belt, and now
at this point with my brother, she is to get her way. We
went out and she was on my last nerve the entire night.
Adam called as we were leaving and threatened me to
where my brother could hear it. He was livid. He drove to
the apartment Adam was staying in that I left, and Adam
knew he was coming for him. Adam and Adam Jr. were
nowhere in sight and mattresses were placed blocking the
doors. The next day I called Adam to tell him I would be
picking Adam Jr. up and he advised me that he didn't have
him. I searched for a week for my son because Adam had
hidden him at one of his workers houses so that I could
not have him. This was a form of abuse and control. I
finally found him and the guy he left him with, had just

SUCK IT UP CUPCAKE, IT'S JUST WITHDRAWAL

gotten out of prison for attempted murder. A couple days later, Adam filed for temporary custody until I got out of residential, but I refused to go because this psycho was not keeping my son. I ended up not going to residential, after a long battle with the courts, and luckily the anti-psychotic kept me from going, because it wasn't allowed in the facility. Adam was awarded temporary custody, so I went back to him because for one, I couldn't stomach being at my brother's house with Lisa, and two, I could have my son every day. Adam claimed in court I was temporarily unable to care for him, but yep, you guessed it, he left Adam Jr. with me every day. It was a complete and total control move and he won, for now.

Somehow Adam's finances where getting better. We moved into an upscale housing community in an adjoining town, that was a guarded community on a lake. The house, although needing work, was situated on a double lot on the water, so the value of the house was around $500,000.00. Adam also acquired, somehow again, a 42-foot Fountain racing boat. He had said that his mentor, friend, and I am still not sure what else he was to Adam, Darius, had let him buy the boat on a payment plan. At this point he had already lost the cell phone store and his Buy Here Pay Here lot was more like a junk yard, so it really didn't make sense how he was able to have these

SUCK IT UP CUPCAKE, IT'S JUST WITHDRAWAL

things. I had gone into the prosecutor's office to meet with him, to discuss things about my case. I thought it was weird he had asked to schedule a meeting with me, but still, at this time, I was naive and in a fog. We talked, and he had shown me a wanted picture on the wall, and asked if I had ever seen the man before. The picture on the poster was of a man in his early thirties, with shaggy brown hair and the name Derrick Baxter. I said "no, should I?" He then told me the story I had been longing to hear for quite some time now. He went on to tell me that Derrick was Adam's business partner and best friend. Derrick used his car dealership as a front to smuggled cocaine into town. Derrick had a warrant out for him for attempted murder of his fiancé, because she had found out what Adam and he were doing. Yes, Adam was a part of it too, and he owned a car dealership. Derrick had been on the run for several years, and they felt that Adam knew where he was. "I will keep an eye out and be more observant, but at this point I have not even heard his name, but know that Adam is very secretive," I told him. I left, going home to confront Adam about what I had been told, and get down to the bottom of things. This is when all hell broke out, beginning my journey of being a battered woman.

Page 55

SUCK IT UP CUPCAKE, IT'S JUST WITHDRAWAL

I was going to my parents' house all day while Adam would go to work. He worked from sun up, to sun down, and even later, and I was ok with it because that meant that I wasn't being ridiculed or yelled at. My father was going in for an experimental treatment for his leukemia, and we were all headed to the hospital. Kendal was in school and Adam Jr. was going to daycare. I was also working here and there at Adams car lot, while I was also attending an outpatient drug treatment program, so it was kind of hard to hold down a job at this point. We arrived at the hospital and my father was put into a hospital room in the cancer wing. They started the treatment and all of a sudden, he flat lined. His potassium level had sky rocketed and we thought he was gone. They called a Code Blue to his room, and doctors and nurses started coming out of the walls running to his room. He was able to stabilize but not after sending me into a horrific panic attack. For anyone who has not had a panic attack, know that they are one of the scariest things you can go through. Your vision goes blurry; your body goes weak. The tightness in your chest along with trouble breathing and heart palpitations, with a side of feeling faint is just plain awful. If you don't know what is happening, you are sure you are dying. This was my first one and I think I aged ten years with it. My entire family was there, they were so supportive and close. You could just see the fear on all of my aunts and uncles faces. That was also the start of a decline in my mother. Her and my father had been married for over thirty years, and she literally could not function without him. The nurses allowed us to go into the room with him, and like always, he started joking and talking about football. This was just the type of man he was. When I went off pain pills, he advised me to go run up and down the road for a while and shake it off. I wished I were that strong. I was weak, not only from weighing a mere 125 pounds and looking anorexic, but my will was weak too. He came home a few days later, but was so frail and a thin, worn version of the man he used to be. I hid the abuse from him because I knew he couldn't handle more than I had already given him.

Adam would come and pick us up at my parents' house very late at night. Kendal was going to school where I had gone, so she would just get off the bus there, and it was convenient. At this point Adam also acquired a new Corvette from Darius, and I am just baffled but have an idea of how he is paying for everything. I would make him go and change cars to drive us home in, so that the kids could have seatbelts on, because a corvette doesn't have rear seats. I was mad at myself for a long time for allowing us to ride with him, when he was drinking, but again did

SUCK IT UP CUPCAKE, IT'S JUST WITHDRAWAL

nothing about it because I felt I had no clout. When we would fight, I would accuse him of being a drug dealer and he would bounce my head off the floor. He was drinking one night when he picked us up, and for some reason was feeling sentimental and loving. He often fluctuated his emotions like this, so I just listened to his sad story as we sat around a bomb fire when we got home. He explained that Derrick was a good guy, not a drug dealer, and made a fortune from his dealership. He said Derrick's fiancé cheated on him one night, and he accidentally discharged a gun at the ceiling of his garage. He felt that they were looking for reasons to put him in jail, so they were charging him with attempted murder. He then went on to say that Derrick was in Columbus and had a team of attorneys working to clear his name, so that he could come back to town. He added that authorities seized all of his property, keeping it for personal use, and that one judge even drove one of his vehicles on vacation. He stated they had a personal vendetta against him. "So you do have contact with him?" I asked. He changed the subject quickly and went on to apologize about being mean all the time. I wasn't buying what he was selling. The next night while we were at my mom and dad's, I tried calling him all evening because I couldn't get ahold of him. It was very late and I ended up falling asleep in the recliner and the kids on the couch. At around 2 a.m. I heard a knock at the door and it was Adam. He was drunk. He had

SUCK IT UP CUPCAKE, IT'S JUST WITHDRAWAL

been in a bar all night and seriously thought we were going to ride with him. I advised him to go as I cried. He left stopping by the next day to apologize. This is typical behavior with a mentally abusive person, they do bad things to you, and then apologize after, and usually your so tore down and in love, that you believe they are truly sorry, but I was starting to wise up. I looked through his phone that day and sure enough in his contacts was Derrick. I called the number and a man answered so I hung up. The next day Adam screamed at me and then begins the constant threats of, I will end you. By this time, I decided to migrate away from him and things started to begin happening, like metal pipes lodged in my parent's tires, and an old suburban nearly running my daughter down as she played in the cul-de-sac. I had seen the suburban before and knew Adam was behind it.

My father was very sick and was admitted into the hospital again. Adam had decided to take Kendal and Adam Jr. to Florida for vacation, but funny thing was I wasn't invited. I was almost sure my father wouldn't make it out of the hospital, and I didn't want the kids to be around if something happened. They flew out and I went to stay at the hospital with my dad. My aunt was also visiting, as she often did and while we were talking, my dad warned me not to screw things up with Adam,

SUCK IT UP CUPCAKE, IT'S JUST WITHDRAWAL

because he was a great guy. Inside I am just dying with anger, but still say nothing. My brother knew what he was but we had decided to keep things quiet. I went home and there was a man standing outside of my parent's trailer. He was lurking and I was beginning to get worried. I called the sheriff in an obvious way that the man could see me, and he fled. The next day I was noticing the man everywhere. I drove into town to go tanning and as I was getting out of my mom's van, the man approached me. He advised me that Adam had asked him to put the fear of God in me to get me to back off about Derrick and the things I thought he might be up to. Luckily, and I don't know why, the man didn't hurt me, but boy did that piss me off. He took my kids so that I could be threatened. As I was lying in the recliner late one night, my brother called and told me to get to the hospital because dad had coded, and was going on life support. I flew to the hospital going 90 mph only to be pulled over. I, crying, explained to the Highway Patrol Officer that my father was going to die. He let me go with a warning to slow down and I went on my way. When I arrived at the hospital, my father was in ICU and was brain dead. We spent the night in a hotel across the street and went the next morning to shut the life support off, because we knew my dad did not want to be kept alive by a ventilator. There were so many family members there. We gathered around his bed, as they shut the machine off. It took hours for him to take his last

SUCK IT UP CUPCAKE, IT'S JUST WITHDRAWAL

breath, and when he did, I began to shake. He was gone.
We left the hospital to return home late that night. I had
called Adam and told him not to tell the kids, that I would.
I picked Adam and them up at the airport the next day,
and the first thing out of Adam Jr.'s mouth was "mommy,
where's papal?" I told them he's in heaven now, and they
cried their little eye's out. This is life loss # 9. My biggest
loss of all.

We had the funeral and there was so many people
there it wasn't even funny. My brother at this point would
not give me a decent word and just completely treated me
like a disease. I had stolen a lot of my father's pain pills,
which left him in agony for a few days until he got more,
but still he refused to press charges. I had relapsed. I
couldn't take it; I couldn't take life. I found out a couple of
weeks later that I was pregnant again. Adam was very
mad and accused me of being pregnant by someone else.
He wanted me to get an abortion. I was just done with life
at this point. Adam was living in bars and I had found out
that he was seeing a girl. While four months pregnant, I
took a bunch of pills, this time I wanted to die for a
moment. I lay in the hospital bed disoriented from the
meds beginning to kick in. No inkling of care, of what may
happen to the baby. I was taken to the hospital and
admitted into mental health. How my PO didn't find out I

SUCK IT UP CUPCAKE, IT'S JUST WITHDRAWAL

have no idea. They let me out of the hospital and I went to stay with my mom. I was released from probation early but not after paying a lot of money in fines. I arrived back at mom's one windy day and dropped my purse on the deck. My things blew under the deck so I had to go down and get them. There was a detective's business card and this scared the daylights out of me. I went inside and called him, and he wanted me to come down to the station for questioning, but wouldn't tell me why. I assumed it was about Adam. I advised him that I was at the obstetrician that day, to be put on bed rest, because I had developed intro-uterine growth retardation and was beginning to swell from preeclampsia as well. He told me to give him a call after the baby was born, but I knew I wouldn't. I went into labor a few days later, so I went to the hospital and was ready for delivery. I called Adam but he wasn't too concerned, he didn't want the baby anyway. He eventually showed up and that night I gave birth to Landen, a small 5 lb. 15 oz. baby boy with black hair, and he was actually born healthy. I took him home and was very stressed, having trouble coping with the new baby crying a lot, and two other children, but I managed and got by. Landen was a few weeks' old when the detective I had talked to called me again.

SUCK IT UP CUPCAKE, IT'S JUST WITHDRAWAL

The detective kept calling, so I called my attorney and told him. He called me the next day while I was taking my son to the doctor and advised me, that they have a charge against me of Illegal Processing of a Drug Document, and not to speak to him at all without him present. I had no idea what he was talking about, no recollection what so ever of doing something with a prescription again. A few days went by and I knew I didn't have the money to pay my attorney, so I called the detective like an idiot, hoping he would help me, because he had implied he would on a previous call. He had asked me about the prescription and the doctor that wrote it, and I just rambled on that I don't know, I really didn't. I had been to so many doctors in the past, that all their names just ran together. He gave me specifics, and went on to tell me that he would help me get away from Adam because they knew about everything. That was a little weird. I told him I did it, thinking he was truly going to help me. I cried and pleaded that I had to get away from Adam, and he recorded the call. This, I found out later, as they used the taped confession to indict me on the charge. They had no evidence at all, just the tape. This came to my attention later that day, when I called him and told him he had tricked me and he pretty much said "yes". This was my third strike with the same charge. I thought I was done for. The incident happened in November, I was charged in June of the next year. When I went to the police station

SUCK IT UP CUPCAKE, IT'S JUST WITHDRAWAL

with my attorney, they asked me if I would turn on Adam or try and get Derrick to come in to town so they could arrest him. I said no way. Adam or Derrick will kill me or hurt my daughter, so you can just charge me. They did. I went home and Adam came over. I told him they wanted me to turn on him and he then tried to grab Landen and take off. Oh, hell no. I pushed him back and he fell against a rocking chair and broke it. He got up, grabbed me by my arms, and threw me across the room to land on my head. I went to grab the phone and he ran out. I called my attorney and he advised me to go into Project Woman. The next day I went, and they put me up in protective custody. Bruises on my arms and all. I took all of the kids, and that was the first day that I decided to turn my life around, but had reserves, because I thought I was going to prison. The next day, I called mental health to get into counseling, and they suggested I do Transitions which is group therapy. The liaison for the police and project woman met with me and wanted me to tell the police all I knew, and even mentioned witness protection. I just couldn't because of my kids. I was in project woman for a couple weeks, and when I would get picked up to go somewhere, I noticed that the police and sheriffs were always following me. When we would turn a corner on a road, one would take over, where the other would leave off. My attorney called me a few days after I left Project

SUCK IT UP CUPCAKE, IT'S JUST WITHDRAWAL

Woman, because I had just had enough of the confinement, telling me that Adam had filed an Emergency Ex Parte Order for custody, saying the children were in danger with me. Luckily the judge disagreed and called for us both to meet in his chambers. This is when the custody battle from hell began. This also began a long hard road for myself, and I knew it was time to get myself and my life back, so I hit my knees and told God, that if he would take me out of this, I would live the rest of my life by him and him alone.

SUCK IT UP CUPCAKE, IT'S JUST WITHDRAWAL

CHAPTER 6-ROCK BOTTOM, THE BEST THING THAT EVER HAPPENED TO ME

By this time, Adam was facing a couple domestic violence charges because of threatening me so much. I was really tired of it. I was filing a civil protection order because he had goons coming by my house, starting fights, and when I showed up at court, he thought it was to spill the beans on him, so he and one of his workers, drove by several times. It was time for my sentencing and I was a nervous wreck at this point. My mother gave me a quarter of one of her benzos before, and it was awful. It was like a bad drunk and I was tired now. I showed up at court with my attorney and stood in front of the judge. He had just asked for Bill Stevens, my previous probation officer to attend. This was a little bit of relief because I thought to myself, why is he having someone from probation come if

SUCK IT UP CUPCAKE, IT'S JUST WITHDRAWAL

he's not going to put me on probation again. He stated I pleaded no contest. I had no idea if I did it or not at this point, but had no memory of it. We stood before the judge as my attorney explained that I had relapsed because I went back into an unhealthy relationship, but was now fighting for custody in the same court, and just started a pretty decent job in Columbus. I was hired for an accounts receivable position making more than I ever had before. The judge gave me a very long lecture and then sentenced me to four years' probation, three years' license suspension, a $5000 fine and 120 days on house arrest. This may sound horrifying to most, but it was like winni9ng the lottery to me. I made up my mind that God lead that judge to give me my second chance, and I was going to run with it. Mr. Stevens was hard core and I knew I had to keep my nose clean and straighten my shit up, because this incident actually occurred while I was on probation from the previous charge. How in the world am I not going to prison? Another stipulation of my probation was that I was not to be on the internet at all. This was because I had always ordered my pills online. They put the hose to me but they let me off pretty much. Either way, I took this as a sign that God listened to my plea, and answered my prayers.

SUCK IT UP CUPCAKE, IT'S JUST WITHDRAWAL

Our court dates for custody were coming up, and my aunt had called my mother to tell her that Adam's picture was in the paper, for the cities most wanted, for a crime of selling motor vehicles without a license. Oh, my God, I was a little happy, wrong, that was, but this showed to the child custody judge and guardian ad litem that Adam was a criminal. The town's most wanted at that. Keep in mind while all of this is going on, I have a feeling that something is going on behind the scenes that I don't know about. We went for our pretrial hearing and the judge ordered that we are to exchange the boys every other day until the final hearing, so that they will get to have equal time with each parent. This was ridiculous considering Landen was about three months old and needed his mother. I had no choice even though I voiced that I did not want his abusive rear end around my children. The judge didn't like that at all. Time went on and with visitations, Adam was already dropping them off late or picking them up at different times, and just blatantly not following the courts set times for exchanges. He also refused to give me the kids clothes from his house as the judge had ordered him to. One day Adam, late again, dropped the kids off and had a girl with dark brown straight hair, in the car with him. My side of the bed isn't even cold at this point and he is already introducing someone new to the boys, and taking her to the lake. I didn't care about him being with someone because I never

SUCK IT UP CUPCAKE, IT'S JUST WITHDRAWAL

truly loved him, he was my enabler. He was an ATM to me and nothing more, but I did care about him somewhat, for he was the father of my children, no matter how I hated him so. The morning of the civil protection hearing, I arrived by myself. Adam came in late and had a young girl about six or seven years old with him. I found out it was his new girlfriend's daughter going to testify how nice he was. First off, what kind of mother lets her daughter go with a man she just met, who has domestic violence charges against him, and is going to a hearing, where his previous woman is filling to keep him legally away from her. Protection is even in the name. My attorney convinced me to agree to a mutual protection order, as I was reserved, but agreed. This means that he could get me in trouble if I go near him. My fear was he was going to take advantage of that. At this time, I had enough of living in a mobile home with my mother, and was ready to start bettering myself in every way. I found a nice country home to rent, and myself, my three children, and my mother all moved in. She couldn't afford to live alone anyway at the time, since my dad was gone, and this would help her out too. I now had a house and a really good job, but was still to face the custody hearing and remain on probation for years.

SUCK IT UP CUPCAKE, IT'S JUST WITHDRAWAL

I was on month three of my house arrest. Adam Jr. had eaten a corn dog and was playing when he started having chest pains. When I got off the pain pills, I developed OCD like no other. My kids would sneeze and they went to the doctor. I called my PO and asked if I could take him to the ER. The kids were scheduled to go with their dad that night at 6 p.m., and it was around 4:30 p.m. when I took him. We were waiting forever when Adam's new girlfriend had walked in with his mother to get the kids. Emily, baby's daddy's new boo, was pregnant. I try and talk gangster but I am the most prim and proper woman you will ever come across, so bear with me. That's what my gangster friends tell me. It gets old being boring sometimes. She also had long blonde curly hair and looked just like me. Freaks me out to this day. People would see her and then ask me why I was with Adam. She changed her appearance to look just like me. She walked into the hospital room and the shit got real. She went to the nurse and said "my mother has been in the medical field for 25 years and it does not take this long for someone to be seen". Holy shit, my ex knocked up Satan's sister. She was horrifying. She grabbed Landen's arm and pulled him away from me, hitting his head on the wall. It took every last bit of composer I had not to choke her out right there. The nurse came in to discharge Adam Jr. and Emily, very snotty like, told the nurse she wanted a copy of all of the paperwork. I asked why, because she

SUCK IT UP CUPCAKE, IT'S JUST WITHDRAWAL

didn't take him to the hospital. She didn't pay for it and neither did her new man. I told the nurse to just give her the paperwork I had already signed, because apparently, she needed to read how to dose Motrin. Emily really did make a fool of herself. As we were leaving the nurse looked at me and said "good luck with that one". I smiled and said "thank you, I think I am going to need it". I walked to my car and she was outside standing, and started taking my picture. Keep in mind this was the first time I had met this girl. I had never ever done anything to her, other than be her new man's ex. She was going to try and show my probation officer that I was not at home. Stupid girl, with house arrest they know the second you leave the perimeter and they come get you. I advised her that I had permission so she can call who ever she wanted to. Since we had the protection order in play, she was going to be doing all of the picking up and dropping off. I could only communicate with her. I wouldn't call this life loss #10 as much as, yes, God gave me a second chance, but he's also giving me a reminder of all the bad things I did during my addiction. I had to take the good with the bad, and Oh my God she was such a cunt! She proved to me over the years that I had 100% control over my emotions, because I did not smack the stupid right out of her. Thought about it daily, but would never act. I would get solace in the fact that when she would come to pick up the boys, Landen went into psycho mode kicking and

SUCK IT UP CUPCAKE, IT'S JUST WITHDRAWAL

screaming. He turned into a damn octopus. How does a little person have that much strength being able to stop you from putting them in a car? Later, I would find out why he hated and feared her so. I answered the phone at work often when the receptionist wasn't able to. Which was a lot. I answered the phone one day at work, and sure enough it was Emily asking if I was available. I said "this is her," and she hung up the phone. And now begins her obsession.

It was time for the final custody hearing and I was a nervous wreck. With my previous meeting with the guardian ad litem, I was crying, because he tore me apart. I had no idea when he was called to the stand that he would recommend me as the custodial parent, but he did. Emily was called to the stand and tried to make her and Adam look like rich saints, but she did it by lying, a lot, and was called out on it. The things she said were a contradiction to what she had told the guardian ad litem. I caught on to it so my attorney confronted her with it. She had told the guardian ad litem that she hadn't drank in years. I had a picture from Myspace showing her drinking just four months earlier. She stated that she made $52,000.00 a year working for Adam. She was asked by my attorney what she did and she stated she uploaded cars onto his web site and it took about six hours a week.

SUCK IT UP CUPCAKE, IT'S JUST WITHDRAWAL

"So you make $166.00 an hour?" he asked. She fumbled for words. He asked her how she got paid and she replied with a W-2. He asked her where she cashed it. My attorney asked her why she had called my PO to tell him I had a Myspace account. "Where you trying to get her sent to prison and taken from the boys?" Of course, she said no. She royally screwed Adam. He was on the stand next and gave the impression he didn't want me near the boys or in their life. Big no no. He also stated he had never been arrested. Hello Tweetal Dumb, you were on the front page of the paper for most wanted. It was then my turn to testify and all I did was tell the truth. I made Adam's attorney look stupid. Emily was smacking Landen and had left marks on his arm. They were making a huge deal of me dating even though it had only dated one guy. I said "I have only dated one guy, but you better believe, any guy I date or marry, better never lay their hands on one of my three kids". His attorney didn't know what to say. My daughter testified the hatred she had for him. Adam's attorney subpoenaed my mother hoping to catch us in lies but nope, she verified everything that I stated. This is just a glimpse of the things that were discussed but you get the idea. I had put Adam Jr. in counseling, paying for it on my own. This was brought up as well and when asked why I put him in, I replied "because he learned to be abusive from his father, and manipulative from me".

SUCK IT UP CUPCAKE, IT'S JUST WITHDRAWAL

Again, I was very honest, even if it made me look bad. My brother testified how much I had changed. When we were leaving, I asked my attorney what he thought. 'He looks squeaky clean and like a bad dad, and you look like a good mother who had a drug problem." A little time went by and I received a phone call on a Wednesday from the school secretary at Adam Jr.'s school. I knew her very well from when I went there. She asked if it was ok for Adam to pick up Adam Jr. because he had papers stating that he had visitations on Wednesdays after school. I said "what papers". She stated they were custody papers and that I had gotten custody. I screamed and said "yes that's fine". I called everyone I knew, and yelled it from the parking lot, that I had won. This was the greatest accomplishment of my life, and I knew God was working behind the scenes to help me, so I had to live an amazing life from here on out. So, begins life after addiction.

SUCK IT UP CUPCAKE, IT'S JUST WITHDRAWAL

CHAPTER 7-CAN'T TOUCH THIS

Working at T L Baxter was nothing short of stepping into a zombie apocalypse with nothing more than a stick of gum to fight off the flesh eaters. The owner's son, Brandon, and I became good friends, but he had something else on his mind. I told him that I was taking the next couple years to stay single, to find myself. This line works great on guys that ask you out when you don't want to go. The cat calls from the shop workers were

SUCK IT UP CUPCAKE, IT'S JUST WITHDRAWAL

Crazy, but we all developed a friendship, and I would just laugh it off, in the beginning. I had gotten Botox and Juviderm because my addiction had me looking a little old and worn out. I was looking great after. I had extensions that I had for several years, but they had forced me to cut a lot of my hair off because the glue was matted. I had fresh ones put in and was looking fly. In the beginning, Brandon was so sweet, and kind, and all he wanted to do was help me out as a friend, because let's face it, being a single mom of three kids was expensive. It's not as hard as it seems though. I was feeling great, the depression had completely gone and I felt as if life was finally going in the right direction, after my house arrest was up of course. Aint no happiness when you're on lock down. Work had no idea of my criminal record. It wasn't on the application and I was never asked, so I didn't volunteer the information. Things were going pretty well at work. I had built up a respect and a lot of friendships. Brandon had started saying things that were a little out of line. I would just smile and brush it off, then the emails started. You look nice today, then your butt looks nice today. This went on for a while until there were hundreds of emails that had been exchanged between us. In the beginning, harmless, in the end, full blown sexual harassment. He was the owner's son for the love of God, how could I put a stop to this without losing my job. I let it go on for a

SUCK IT UP CUPCAKE, IT'S JUST WITHDRAWAL

couple years, and one day he asked me to go into the women's bathroom, so that he could show me how a woman should feel. Gulp! After this I started deterring him more and explained to him why I didn't want to be with any guys at the time. He was in love. We continued to email and one day he asked me why the hell I was on a dating site. My friend had put me on one. Who the hell wants a five-time felon as a wife? I never got on it so it was unimportant to me. His complete attitude just changed from that day forward. He started bossing me around a little bit, and then, sent the email. It read something along the lines of my daddy owns this place and unless you want to lose your job, you better this and you better that. Oh, no no little boy. He was 12 years younger than me, so to me he was a little boy. I took the letter to our GM, who I had built a wonderful professional relationship with, and showed it to him. Brandon was suspended for a week from work with no pay, after being written up. And then comes, retaliation.

Most of the people at work were great, I adored them, then you had Brandon and Caleb. Caleb was young and would cut just about anybody's throat to get ahead. He lied constantly and would tell on people even with it being things that were not true. Then he would try and act like he was your best friend. Yes, one of those people.

SUCK IT UP CUPCAKE, IT'S JUST WITHDRAWAL

He and Brandon would always whisper when they were around me, like they were up to something. My good friend at work, Kandy, was getting tired of Caleb's antics as well, and they would go round, and round, and she would put him in his place. I loved it. They were always doing something to me, be it remote accessing my computer, or telling the owner I did something. It was very stressful but at this point I could handle stress. It was the weirdest thing, it's like I got a lot stronger and smarter from being with Adam. I had learned how to be an adult, and handled things, like an adult would. Brandon, when written up, was also moved upstairs to an office away from my desk. They really did take the right punishment measures so I was not worried about anything at this point. I complained a few times and Brandon would get a warning. I let both Brandon and Caleb know that I was aware of them remote accessing my computer, and disabled it, on several occasions. Work was starting, at this point, to unravel very slowly. I bought a used Ford Expedition and my payments were pretty high. I didn't make that much at my job and should have never bought it, but I did because I could. At this time in my life, I was mostly worried about appearances, which was another downfall of mine. Before this job, I had bartended for a while and was complimented constantly, even being told I should be on TV. I was oozing with confidence. I was getting my life turned around finally, and it felt amazing. Other than

SUCK IT UP CUPCAKE, IT'S JUST WITHDRAWAL

dealing with kids at work, things were pretty good, but I felt as if something was missing. I knew I kept telling guys, I didn't want to date, but was that the truth? "You can find yourself, and still be in a relationship," I thought. But there was that record I had to deal with, and being on probation. I was pretty good at hiding it from work, but could I hide it from a partner? I was sitting at work one day and my truck was repossessed. I had to make more money, my job wasn't paying enough, and do I really want to stay working with these guys that won't leave me alone? I decided, I'm going back to school. I enrolled at a community college to study Social Work, and Chemical Dependency Counseling. This would prove to everyone that I have turned my life around completely. I now have a plan for the future.

I would date a guy here, and there, but never would introduce them to the boys. I dated some really hot guys, but every one of them would end our relationship, because I put my children first. I also developed a little bit of an issue, I became controlling. I was so out of control for so many years, that at this time, I had to have complete order. Schedules, routines and following an agenda where key to my days running smoothly. I never really wanted to get too close to someone though, because of my criminal history. A few years prior to this point, while I was at a

SUCK IT UP CUPCAKE, IT'S JUST WITHDRAWAL

softball game, I had run into the brother of one of my good friends. There were three brothers, all of which I had grown up with since I was around eight, but after graduation, had lost touch with. He stated that Jared, the youngest brother, was in Iraq working as a civilian contractor. I told him, to tell Jared, to give me a call when he came home, so we could go do something and hang out. I never heard from him, so I forgot all about it. At this time, after losing touch for a little while, Anna, my good best friend, and I, began doing things together because I now, was not under lock and key with Adam. She had for years wanted a divorce from her husband, but up until then had not filed. Her husband had gotten another girl pregnant, again, so she decided to go through with it. We had so much fun together and started a new tradition that involved just the two of us. Party on the porch. Rain or shine, freezing or hot, we would drink a bottle of tequila on the porch. It was the funniest thing ever. We continued this tradition for years. We dated t3o guys tht were best friends, but never really clicked with them. I had become so picky. The perspective I took was, would I want these guys in my children's life. Kendal was so easy going and her dad didn't really care about anything but himself, so it was easy dating with her, but with the boys, I was under the magnifying glass on just breathing, let alone bringing a man around the boys. I got a message one night from Jack, he was Jared's middle brother. He gave me

SUCK IT UP CUPCAKE, IT'S JUST WITHDRAWAL

Jared's number, so I called him to see what he was up to. He was sitting with his girlfriend just hanging out. At this point he had been back from Iraq for several years, and we had a lot to talk about. He told me they were going to a bar the next night and asked if I would like to join. I told him that Anna and I would probably stop in to see them, but the bar was kind of a dive, so I told him we wouldn't be staying long. At this point I am a very blunt person too. No lies or sugar coating, and definitely no filter. I called Anna and she agreed to go.

Anna and I walked into the bar and found Jared playing pool. We hugged and he looked really good. He was such a cutie. He then brought his girlfriend over to meet us and oh my God, she was a stick wearing Barbie's bikini top with jeans with red high heels. Was she a prostitute? Anyway, we hung out for a while with Jared, Colleen his girlfriend, and Luke, Jared's best friend from childhood. I guess I went to school with Luke, but I had my head up my butt so I don't recall. Luke thought I was a bitch, but kept it to himself, because we talked like we had known each other for years. All he did was complain about Colleen getting Jared on Heroin. Wait, What? Turns out Colleen turned Jared on to it and they were using a lot, and regularly. We left and went to another bar. Everyone was three sheets to the wind by the end of the night and

SUCK IT UP CUPCAKE, IT'S JUST WITHDRAWAL

you could tell there was some type of animosity between Jared and Colleen, but I just passed it off as liquor. On our way home Anna and I couldn't believe who he was dating, she looked like a crack head, and then we talked about how good Jared looked. After this we all went out a few more times, and it was a constant argument with the two love birds, but at this point it was expected and dismissed. I talked to Jared and we were to meet him at the same bar later that evening. Jack went with me and as I walked into the bar, a girl walked up to me and said "Kerri bleeping Cavalier, what are you doing here?" I had no clue who this rude, lunatic was, and looked to Colleen for answers. Collen just said "Cheryl, that was high school." We went to high school together? I guess I was a bitch. I walked away and started talking to Jared, and Jack just advised me that this Cheryl was bat shit crazy and to ignore her. Jack and I left and I didn't think more about it. Couple days later, Jared called and asked if I wanted to go for a Harley ride, I asked him what about Colleen, and he stated they broke up. I agreed and went to Jared's apartment. He told me he was on heroin and had just gotten clean, and I told him I was proud of him, but I'm not going to condemn or judge him. I asked him what his withdrawal was like. He said that he would just throw up after he drank his morning coffee. Seriously? I felt that I was living inside of a bug zapper and you get off with a woozy stomach. Maybe it's because he is a 220 lb. man with nerves of

SUCK IT UP CUPCAKE, IT'S JUST WITHDRAWAL

steel, I don't know, but I was envious. Withdrawal truly does affect everyone different. We left on the bike, and as I was petrified holding on to the back of him, he made a comment about kissing. I said "no way, because you're like my little brother."   He said "whatever," and we went bar to bar. I had the best time I had in a long time. I think I was crushing on him, and today have no idea why I didn't act on it that night. That all changes.

About a week later, I talked to Jared through text, and he said to go to The Barn, the bar we had always went to. I showed up with Jack and sure enough, Cheryl greeted me, and not in a nice way. She asked me what I was doing riding bikes with Jared. Jared pulled her aside to tell her to back off, as Colleen came up to me. Wow, they are together. Colleen told me she called Jared to get back together, because she was told by several people that Jared was riding bikes with a really pretty girl on the back. This girl is unreal. I told her it was just me. She said she knows that now, and we went on to have a good time singing karaoke and playing darts. Luke was there and complained of Colleen the whole night. This would have been understandable had Luke not snorted every drug he could get his hands on. We left and went bar hopping, and sure enough Jared and Colleen fought the entire night. A couple days later Jared came to help me move

SUCK IT UP CUPCAKE, IT'S JUST WITHDRAWAL

a couch, and Colleen came with him. We were sitting in the garage talking, and Colleen was telling me how she was on buprenorphine because she was getting clean from the heroin. This chick was drooling and slurring. She was abusing it now, as many opiate addicts do. This is the reason along with my cold turkeys, that I felt this was a drug that was not needed. It just seemed like a wimp's way out to me. Jared and my brother talked for a bit while I tried counseling Colleen, but I could truly see that she was in fact, a junkie. I didn't even slur when I would take six or seven hydrocodone, so what was she taking? They left, and over the next few months Jack and I had hung out a lot. In this time, I had met Wesley, and boy was he madly in love with me at the first moment he saw me. He was pretty well off as he drove a new BMW and lived in a three-story condo in a ritzy part of Columbus. He would take me everywhere I wanted to go. He tried to take me on several vacations but I couldn't go and leave my children, that is one thing I never did at this point, was to leave them other than going to work. Wesley and I had hot steamy sex with no connections. He seemed too much of the perfect bachelor for me to introduce my kids to anyway, so we just stuck with a casual relationship.

I would go to Wesley's house every other weekend unless Jack and I decided to do something. Sometimes

SUCK IT UP CUPCAKE, IT'S JUST WITHDRAWAL

Jack went with me to Columbus to see Wesley, and the three of us went out. Jack was such a good friend, we had a brother, sister relationship, and he treated me like gold, even taking care of me with a puke pan before I would throw up on his floor, after I drank way too much. Jack had told me that Jared was moving to Maryland to start over. He had ended it with Colleen because he didn't want to live that life anymore. He moved in with a friend of ours from high school who got him hired at his job making really good money. I would miss him but was glad for him to be out of that lifestyle. I ran into Colleen's mother at a union club in town and she had told me that Jared had beat up Colleen and fled the state. Please, he wouldn't put his hands on a woman, even your junkie daughter. I knew this was a fictitious junkie story being told, so I laughed and walked away. Her mother was an old bar fly anyway. Cheryl was there with her that night, but we actually had a decent conversation and I thought I just might like this girl. I called Jack the next day and told him what her mother had said, and he told me that Jared had lost everything to his and Colleen's addiction and he had to move away from it. When he was in Iraq he made over $400,000.00, and they had snorted it all away. Colleen started stealing and sleeping with her dealer and Jared left and never looked back, until he came back for a Memorial day party at his mom's house. He called me to come and I showed up with a guy friend of mine and my

SUCK IT UP CUPCAKE, IT'S JUST WITHDRAWAL

mother. We were going out and just stopped by for a minute to give hugs. We stayed for a half hour and I left thinking nothing more. He called again on July 1st, and said he was going to his dad's house at Indian Lake, and asked if I would like to go. I said I could but my daughter and her new boyfriend, Redtick, were going to be with me, so he said to bring them too. Justin is his real name, he got that nickname Redtick, from raising redtick hound dogs. He was quite a few years older than Kendal, but he was a really good guy and I didn't see a problem with it, plus I read all of their texts. I went to pick Jared up at his moms, and we all headed to the lake. His brothers were there, along with his older brother's family and his dad and step-mom. They were the nicest people. So polite and kind. We all drank beer and had a really good time. This was July 3rd, and we were up there for the 4th. The next day we all played corn hole and boated and again drank a lot. The neighbor was having a bonfire, so we all walked down to visit, then they broke out the crown. They gave it to Redtick and he drank a lot of it. Jared asked me to walk back to the house with him to get more beer, so I did. We loaded the cooler and started walking back over to their house. He grabbed my arm and pulled me to him. He kissed me. It lasted a long time. I had never felt that way when someone had kissed me before. It was like all of the cares of the world just melted away. When we finished, we both laughed and I said "guess you're not like

SUCK IT UP CUPCAKE, IT'S JUST WITHDRAWAL

my little brother anymore," and he responded "thank God". This moment changed my life forever, good and bad. We spent the 4th making our own fireworks and just really became so close that it was as if we shared the same soul. We went to his mom's and spent the night in my truck by a camp fire, and the next day he came home with me. I had a get together with my daughter and her friends, and as I was sitting on Jared's lap he looked at me and said "I want to say I love you so bad". We had been together for three days. I responded "then go ahead." I felt it too. This begins my fourth relationship, and what I hope will be my last, and with that I mean forever lasting.

SUCK IT UP CUPCAKE, IT'S JUST WITHDRAWAL

CHAPTER 8-WILL THE REAL LOVE OF MY LIFE PLEASE STAND UP

Jared was still living in Maryland at this point and was making the drive back to stay at my house every weekend. Martin, our friend that he was living with, said that he made up so many excuses to come back to Ohio it wasn't even funny. I think three family members died. Jared was infatuated and he showed it. Jared told me he couldn't take it and had to move back. I let him move in

SUCK IT UP CUPCAKE, IT'S JUST WITHDRAWAL

with us and he left a great job behind, only to come to Ohio and be jobless. We didn't care, we were so in love. He moved in and my kids absolutely adored him. We were one big happy family with a live-in mother in law for Jared. He was so great about that. At this time, I was taking my first chemical dependency class once a week on Wednesdays. I was sitting in class, and received a text from my brother, to call him immediately. I stepped out of the room and into the hall to call him. He said that children's services stopped by our house and talked to my mother, and wanted me to call them. Do what? I take amazing care of those kids, why would someone call children's services on me? The next day I called and talked to a gentleman who said he needed to come do a home visit, because there had been close to 20 anonymous calls made on me. Just two days before Emily had text me wanting to know all of Jared's information, so she could do a background check on him, and advised me that they needed to know everything about him. Stupid, stupid girl, it's none of your business. I advised her he had no criminal record, and that I had known him my whole life, unlike her and Adam knowing each other two weeks and moving in together. I knew that the calls were from her and Adam. Remember, I have a civil protection order in place at this time, and Adam and I cannot have any contact with each other, so I have to converse with Godzilla over everything about the boys. Greg, from

SUCK IT UP CUPCAKE, IT'S JUST WITHDRAWAL

children's services came to the house and we sat down
and talked. He advised me of the complaints and I was
flabbergasted. Just to name a few; the boys having
pruned hands from swimming too much, I was sleeping
naked with my new boyfriend and the boys in the bed with
me, I was giving Adam Jr. cough syrup for a tooth ache, our
house was filth because of a new puppy we had and the
list of bull shit went on. As Greg and I sat and I proved to
him everything they called about was a lie, he pulled me
outside, off the record, and said Adam needed knocked
down to size. I had already explained to him the things
that Adam had done to me, and he instantly didn't like
him. By God's grace, he saw the truth, like our custody
judge had, and left on good terms.

About two weeks later I was walking through my
front room and saw a sheriff parked in my drive way. It
was about 11 o'clock at night and I was a nervous wreck.
Just a little bit before this, Adam called Adam Jr.'s phone
while he was in the bath tub, and I answered it. The caller
ID said Emily. It was Adam saying in a very rude tone "let
me talk to Jr." I advised him he was busy and hung up the
phone, since we weren't supposed to be talking, so again I
knew, they were why the sheriff was there. He was a tall,
fairly built sheriff, who had a look of intimidation

on his face. I start ranting that he called and it said Emily, and I answered it. I then said how I filed the protection order because he was a drug dealer, and Derrick this, and car dealership that. I was ranting. After a bit, he too became very understanding and pissed at Adam. He checked on the boys who were fast asleep in my bed, and then stated he was going to go call Adam, and that if he were pressing charges against me, that he was going to jail too. "I'll drive to his house and pick him up myself," he said. He went to the car and called. A few minutes later he called me to tell me that Adam had just requested a well check on the boys. He advised me if he does one more thing, to call him and he will handle it. I graciously thanked him. One thing I forgot to mention was that during the custody battle, Emily filed a false police report on me for phone harassment. I was able to show that sheriff, that she was in fact calling me. Even had my phone records to prove it. I called Emily and explained to her that sending children's services and sheriffs to my house on false calls was a violation of the civil protection order and if it doesn't stop, they both were going to jail. Have you ever despised someone so much that it makes your stomach churn just by thinking of them? Emily was this to me. She would always start a fight when getting the boys, and it was getting out of hand. I was always so

SUCK IT UP CUPCAKE, IT'S JUST WITHDRAWAL

polite and nice, because I was on probation and she had already tried to send me to prison once. She even showed up once and started rattling off about how she had an 850-credit score. You're so full of shit Emily, is what I would think to myself. Well one day she brought the boys home and Landen was a mess. I asked Adam Jr. what happened to him and he advised me that Emily was forcing suppositories up his rectum and hurting him. I could feel the anger manifest into a fever, my ears were red, and I couldn't concentrate. Apparently, Landen had pooped and got it on her wall, so she went ballistic on him, screaming at him, so he now refused to poop at their house. I called Greg at children's services and asked him what I should do. He advised me to scare the crap out of her. I had to do it in person so there was no way to trace it. I was waiting till she came to pick the boys up next, to threaten her, or just scare the shit out of her. She came, I got in her face, I told her the police were looking for her because she had sexually assaulted Landen. She flipped out. I told her they were waiting on my word to file official charges, and I needed to call them when she leaves. She was begging for me not to. I told her, "I'll tell you what, don't ever put your hands on one of my children again, and don't file one more false report on me, or I would truly make her regret the day she met Adam. I also advised her, all of the government agencies were after Adam, and she will go down with him if I just give them the information I knew.

SUCK IT UP CUPCAKE, IT'S JUST WITHDRAWAL

She said it would stop, and drove off in terror. After this Landon developed a disorder known as Encopresis, from holding going to the bathroom so much. I detest this chick.

Kendal wanted to go to the mall, so Jared and I, along with my mother and Kendal's friends, decided to go and then get something to eat. At this point Jared and I had been together for two months, but it felt as if we were in a relationship much longer, the comfort and ease of things was amazing. As we were walking by a jewelry store, Jared and I looked at each other. I said "let's do it." We went into the store, and he applied for a credit line. He had good credit so was approved for a decent amount, and he bought the most beautiful wedding set. I was on cloud nine. I was wearing that thing with pride. Kendal needed to buy something else in the mall, so everyone but her and I went across the street to Frickers. Her and I arrived shortly after to the entire bar yelling congratulations. I was like what the what. Jared went in and announced to everyone that he had just gotten engaged. "I just got engaged," he kept saying with a smile. We ate and went home for the evening. That night we combined our Facebook pages because it's not official till it's on Facebook. He had me delete mine because I literally had 400 body builders along with about 100 guys

SUCK IT UP CUPCAKE, IT'S JUST WITHDRAWAL

that I had dated. Friends congratulated us and we soaked in the excitement. The boys were with their dad for the weekend so we decided the next day to go to the lake and celebrate alone. When you live with your mother, you get sick of screwing in the bathroom after a while. Actually, we screwed in everyone's bathroom, we couldn't be left alone for five minutes. That's all we did. As we were sitting at the lake house after dinner, I received a text, it was Wesley. Mind you I hadn't talked to Wesley for a while, because he texted me and told me that he loved me one day. I didn't feel the same. I text Jack to ask him what to say to him and Jack said to say "thank you," so I did. I'm an asshole. Why would you tell someone who just poured their heart out to you saying they love you, thank you? Anyway, I told him I was sitting with my fiancé, Jack's brother. He was appalled and he kept saying that's gross. Hold up, Jack was like my brother, he wasn't my actual brother. To this day, seven years later, Wesley will text me or try and call every so many months, despite Jared threatening his life. We enjoyed our weekend at the lake, and headed home. Back to reality we go.

Jared had come back to Ohio without a job so I knew things would be challenging, however, a friend of his was able to get him a job as a fueler at an airport in a few towns east of us. He started out not making much but I

SUCK IT UP CUPCAKE, IT'S JUST WITHDRAWAL

didn't care, besides, we had four incomes in the house. I knew we could make it. One evening when I got home from work, Jared was not there. My mom had not seen him and he was not answering the phone. He had my truck, and I had his car, so that he could fill the gas cans up with fuel, because our house was heated by fuel oil, and we were out. It was the dead of winter. Hours passed and we were all cold. By 9 o'clock that night I was furious. I had called his mother, and Jack, to see where he could be, but he wouldn't answer them either. I got the inkling that he was at The Barn, and drove there. Sure enough, he and Luke were getting drunk at the bar. I walked in and he acted like nothing could be wrong. It's the Adam incident all over again. Luke asked me to sit at the bar and talk. I sat down and he started lecturing me about Jared, what he wants out of life and this and that. Shut the hell up you drunk, was all I could think. I grabbed my keys from Jared and left him his and advised him not to come home. The next day he showed up and I kicked him out. I am not putting up with that bull shit at all. He moved his TV out and went to stay with Luke. At this time, I am starting to feel like Luke is a very jealous person and doesn't want to share Jared. I am feeling that he has a crush on him. A few days went by and I was very sad at this point. I was over being mad, and really starting to miss him. I text him, and for some reason, I was apologizing and asking him to come home. Wait a minute, he screwed up and your

SUCK IT UP CUPCAKE, IT'S JUST WITHDRAWAL

apologizing, what is wrong with you! He came back home and things went back to good like they were before this incident, but financially, we were sinking, because of the cost of the house and keeping up with the utilities. They were outrageous. Jared and I went to Kentucky a few months later on a Wednesday, and were married. Yes, we were married on a weekday and then went to Landen's preschool meeting after. At this point, Adam Jr., who was just used by his father as a weapon in a custody battle, was suffering pretty bad in school. His teacher tried to say he had ADHD, but I knew different with just the little bit of schooling I had already had. A good friend of mine was a real estate agent, and Jared had a pretty good credit score, so I called her and asked her what the process of buying a home was. She advised us to go to a mortgage broker, so we did. Jared was approved to buy a house after a grueling process, and he was good enough to give me free range to find one. I found one in a neighboring town and we began the process. I also had decided at this point to put Adam Jr. in private school, as well as start Landen out at one. A nice little town had a private school and the house that I wanted, so a few months later, we signed the papers for our new house, and began the rehab process as well as set up for the boys to go to St. Mary's Catholic School in the fall. Other than getting custody of the boys, this was the most excited I had ever been.

SUCK IT UP CUPCAKE, IT'S JUST WITHDRAWAL

CHAPTER 9-HAPPY WIFE, HAPPY LIFE

Adam Jr. and Kendal were finishing out the school year in our old district, but we went ahead and started fixing the house to move in. We were moving into the same district as the boy's dad, so it made it easier for them. Not that that made a difference for me. At this point, Emily is trying to be my friend, so I run with it. Peace at last. The house we bought was a foreclosure and it was a mess. My mother and I spent around $7000.00 to completely refurnish it, along with painting and carpet cleaning. We lived in a HOA now, and had many rules we had to follow. It was an amazing neighborhood, with

SUCK IT UP CUPCAKE, IT'S JUST WITHDRAWAL

really nice houses, and it seemed that a police officer or firefighter lived on every corner. We finished the house and it was beautiful. We owned our own home, hell yeah! It was four bedrooms so that my mother could move in with us as well. At this point she was retiring at the end of the school year, and agreed to help with the childcare, in exchange for not really paying any bills except groceries and occasionally helping out if we need her to. We would have Anna or Luke over all the time, and we were just enjoying our new investment. Summer had come and Jared was tired of me spending $20.00 a day on gas for my Expedition to get to work, so he bought a Honda Civic for me to drive. He then went and bought Kendal her first car. Kendal was Jared's baby, whatever she wanted, she got. We had spent a few weekends up at the lake with Jared's family, as well as at Jared's mothers house, because she had an inground pool. The summer came to an end and it was time for the boys to start private school, and Kendal was going to a technical school for firefighting and EMS. My life felt complete. I had a good job, less the drama, we had our own home that was beautiful, we had four cars, my kids, I had custody of, were going to great schools, my husband was obsessed with me and life was a dream. The only thing hovering over my head, was probation. I had dreamed of being at this place in my life, but never thought it would have been possible. Then things started getting a little rocky.

SUCK IT UP CUPCAKE, IT'S JUST WITHDRAWAL

Turns out, psycho Cheryl was Carol, Jared's mother's best friend, despite the huge age difference. Kendal was in 4H, and the first years, raised rabbits to show, and decided she wanted to start doing dairy feeders. Jared arraigned for Cheryl to get and keep a cow for Kendal, and we would just pay for feed, as well as Kendal needed to go over a few times a week to help clean out the stalls. Cheryl and I were becoming cool with each other, so I thought this would be a good idea. I would take Kendal over and she would do more work than anyone there, including Cheryl, Jackson, Cheryl's son, and a couple other kids who kept their cows there. Redtick would go and help Kendal all the time, and one day Cheryl asked them to go to the feed store to help get feed and supplies. At this point I had given Cheryl a couple hundred dollars and knew I needed to give her a little bit more. Redtick came home that night and told me the feed she was getting was molded, and she was getting it for free. Jesus! I told Jared about it but one thing with him is, if it's one of his people, they do no wrong. Annoyed the piss out of me. Luckily, he has truly grown as a man and a person, or else he would be single, living with mommy, and still running the bars and doing every drug ever produced or grown with the exception of crack. I really am surprised his nose hasn't said bleep you, I'm out. Under my breath, I used to call him sniffy snifferson. Cheryl was his buddy. I told Jared that I wasn't going to pay for molded feed that could

SUCK IT UP CUPCAKE, IT'S JUST WITHDRAWAL

kill the cow. He was pissed but nothing more was said about it, until, Cheryl brought Jared's mother into the mix. Things were starting to be said and this is the first taste I was getting of all of their bull shit. Jared called Cheryl and threw me under the bus. Told her I was the one not paying her, and I said this and said that. Are you bleeping kidding me? After he told me this, my feelings for him started changing a bit. I was kind of in shock to be honest. That night Cheryl and Carol went out and got drunk. Carol called me and started the conversation with "I've been drinking and let me tell you this," she started, saying I was talking about Cheryl, and accused her of this then that. I hung up on her and ran down stairs. I was yelling at Jared telling him he had better do something about his fucking mother before I do. I fought a man to survive, I am not scared of some dumb redneck white trash bitch and your mother. I screamed I was so pissed. Jared yelled at me blaming me. I laughed thinking what kind of piece of shit people are you guys? The next day while Jared was sober and thinking straight, he called his mom and advised her she probably wouldn't see us for a long time, that is if I don't divorce him. She called me several times but I wouldn't answer, because I can say things to cut people to their core, to shake and rattle them. I was afraid I would say something that I would regret, and Carol could never

SUCK IT UP CUPCAKE, IT'S JUST WITHDRAWAL

forget. Once again this got swept under the rug, and we moved on. I was still as sweet as can be to everyone.

I was drinking a lot on the weekends. I had always hated beer, but my husband drank it a lot and turned me on to it. I would sometimes get off of work and come home and drink a few, but I didn't make it a habit of doing that because of getting up so early the next morning. I started on a health kick. I had never really been overweight, but I wasn't my ideal weight either. I wanted a bikini body to go with the rest of me. I have always had the flattest stomach even after my children, but struggled with a big butt and flabby thighs. I started getting up early every morning before work, around 5;30 am, and going to the YMCA to walk and work out. I had built up to walking five miles a morning with weights here and there and was starting to look good from the hips down. Never skinny, but just a good size. It was time for my daughter's graduation and we were having it at my mother-in-law's house to utilize the pool and huge yard. I went and found the perfect bikini, along with a white cover up belly top and see through pants to wear over my bathing suit. I had worked hard to look good and everyone else would be wearing bathing suits, why can't I? Jared and I arrived at his mom's house and she was on the riding lawn mower.

SUCK IT UP CUPCAKE, IT'S JUST WITHDRAWAL

"What the fuck is she wearing?" She said to Jared. I had been over a couple days before helping to clean and get ready for the party. I picked thousands of freaking weeds from her pool area to the point I could barely move my legs, I was so sore. She had then said to me that she thought I was going to clean and help get ready for the party, and something along the lines of you can't do that with the way you are dressed. I again ignored the meanness and skimmed the pool, then put up tents and chairs. I don't remember what Jared was doing at this point, but I don't think it was helping. People started arriving and the kids and Jared were just wearing their swimming trunks, and everyone was playing and having a good time. Carol was rude to me the entire party and I noticed her whispering every five minutes to my step sister in law Noreen. I was having fun and brushed it off. Noreen and I went inside and brought the food down to set on the tables, then I went back to cornhole, and she went back to talking about me with Carol. Later that night, Anna and I went into the pool area to sit and talk, and were going to let the kids swim. Jared was being a jerk to me and I had no idea why. Carol came running up and yelling at me in front of everyone. She was telling us no, and being the biggest bitch I have ever seen. I was livid and walked down to the fire to tell Jared I wanted to leave because of his mom. Luckily at this point most people had

SUCK IT UP CUPCAKE, IT'S JUST WITHDRAWAL

cleared out. Jared started screaming at me. Not just yelling, like neighbors three miles away can hear, screaming. We fought and I tried to reason with him on what the hell he thought I did. His mom bleepin followed us everywhere. We were inside fighting and my mom got the boys in the car to leave, she was waiting on me because Jared drove us separate and she knew the shit was on. I walked out to the car and Charley, Jared's step dad was dawging my daughter out. I lose my shit screaming. My throat hurt after. Carol came running to the car and said, "let me ask you this, who paid for Kendal's car," I responded I pay the payments. She then said 'who pays for the boys' private school," again I responded child support. She had nothing, so then said, like a cunt, "your outfit is hideous." I laughed at this point. We started to pull out and I left my lighter on the table, so I got out and looked for it. She wasn't done running her mouth and started telling me to get out of there. I left with only the thought of how much will my attorney cost on Monday. I kid you not, the next morning Jared came home like nothing had ever happened. Maybe he has smoked crack, I don't know at this point. He went to his moms and cleaned up and told her that I had every right to be pissed, they had ganged up on me. As he was telling me this, I was thinking, you bi-polar mother fuckers. She wanted to talk, but again, that's not a good idea. I am still

SUCK IT UP CUPCAKE, IT'S JUST WITHDRAWAL

as kind as can be at this point and keeping my cool. To this day, I haven't lost it with her, but luckily Jared set her straight one day and she has been kind and loving since. My respect and love for Jared is questionable at this point.

At this point in life, my job is driving me nuts, the retaliation is real. I can't breathe without Brandon saying something to me or telling on me. I start getting physically ill on the way to work. I come home and I am just drinking every night. You could tell the stress was getting to me. Luke and I, at this point, are not caring for each other because Jared stopped hanging out with him, he was a drug addict for God sakes. My mother is showing signs every day of being a spoiled brat. She was also lying all the time to people, telling them that Jared and I did things that we never had. She has always liked to play the victim, but it was getting out of control. I am at a breaking point. I would quit drinking here and there and feel like crap for a few days, but nothing dangerous, just a flu like feeling and anxiety. I was also smoking almost, if not, two packs of cigarettes a day. What was happening to me? Jared kept saying I needed to quit drinking because it makes me mean and bitchy. No, psycho, you are drunk every day and I am getting tired of that, and you leaving when you just can't take it anymore. You are a coward. I was missing a lot of work because I just couldn't face going in

SUCK IT UP CUPCAKE, IT'S JUST WITHDRAWAL

every day, and going through that. I'm starting at this point to hide my drinking from the boys, and knowing I am developing a problem. I would at no point, ever drink or drive, so I was relying on my mother to take the boys to practice every evening so I could drink. If I ran out of beer or wine, I would have her run to the gas station for me. Jared and I were fighting everyday just about, and my perfect life was spiraling out of control. Didn't care much in the evenings because I was drinking, but during the day the anxiety was real. I started having problems controlling going number two, meaning it was liquid and I shit my pants at work. This happened a couple times and it was bad. At this point, Kendal drops a bomb on me that she is pregnant and due in October. She knew for a while but also knew I would try and kill her, but she was 18. I also have Emily texting me all the time wanting to run her mouth, then when I prove to her that I am right about whatever bull shit she is talking about, she wants to be friends. Oh, my God, I need a vacation.

Luke was causing trouble again and I was just wearing thin. He came over and Jared was so drunk and as he was going to bed, kissed Luke on the mouth. I was like what the fuck. Understand I know at this point that Luke has the hots for Jared but Jared is oblivious. Jared goes

SUCK IT UP CUPCAKE, IT'S JUST WITHDRAWAL

upstairs and breaks stuff again. Luke left and Jared came downstairs to us fighting again, so he got his keys and was going to leave. He was so drunk I was afraid he would kill someone. I took his keys and the little bitch called the cops on me. Hello, I'm drunk and my wife took my keys, idiot. The cops came and had carol come and get Jared and he left. I blocked Luke's number from his phone. The next day he came back like he had done no wrong, again. His phone rang and it was Justin, Luke's sons phone. Jared answered and it was Luke saying I blocked his number. Jared left me. I would text him and text him wanting him to come back despite how bad he treated me. One morning I was sitting at work and he text me that he's sorry but he doesn't love me anymore. My heart sank and I was broken. It hurt, for about two days. I beg and I begged some more for him to come home. Anna came over quite a bit to help me get my mind off things. I was off probation at this point and had been for a bit, and I think that is why the drinking started, on top of life falling apart. Her and I went out and had such a good time getting hit on. We had a few parties where Jared's friends came. We were living it up and I was having a blast. Jared and I shared a Facebook page and I was sure to post some funny crap with Anna. We talked about how much fun we were having and I really did stop caring about Jared. Then one morning he text me again telling me he missed his family. I rejected him because he asked if I had gotten help. I told him we could be friends and that I was going out to dinner with and ex. He cried and I was glad he did. A couple days later he stopped by and we ended up working things out. I don't know why I couldn't be my strong self that just left men in the dust and went on with my life. It was coming closer to my granddaughter being born so I decided it was time to stop the drinking. I quit a couple days before and had chemically induced anxiety 24/7 for four days. It was so bad it hurt. Finally, I had a day of relief and went to the hospital that night to see Kendal because she was being induced. The next morning, we sat at the hospital all day and besides a little bit of an achy neck, I felt fine. My beautiful granddaughter was born that night and I almost passed out when she arrived. This fear came over me and all I could think of to do is run or pass out. Her dad and his family were there starting drama over who got to see the baby first, it reminded me why I left him. The next day mommy and baby came to stay with me so I could help take care of them while Redtick worked. She had a horrific delivery and I didn't know if she would make it or not. I was missing work all this time so it was no surprise when my boss called me and fired me, on my birthday. This might have just turned out to be one of the best things that could have happen to me.

SUCK IT UP CUPCAKE, IT'S JUST WITHDRAWAL

CHAPTER 10-IT'S A WHALE OF A TALE

I filed for unemployment and just waited. I also went to the Civil Rights Commission. I wasn't taking this lying down. Very shortly here after I started drinking again. I was approved for unemployment, and was actively looking for a job. I received a letter from unemployment that my decision was reversed because my old boss appealed it. I appealed that decision. At this time, I had obtained and attorney. The case was set for a hearing where I would have to face Allen one on one. We went to the hearing very early in the morning. I noticed I was already beginning to start the shaking again from not drinking during the day. I was very fragile talking to Allen and the facilitator of the hearing but I did a really good job. I poured everything out on the table and Allen was second guessing himself right and left. I left there with a feeling of satisfaction, then came home to drink to celebrate. About a week later, I received the decision that I was again, granted unemployment. I also received an email from my attorney that Allen had reconsidered a settlement. I did better than I thought in the hearing. We agreed on a settlement which helped us out significantly considering our finances were always in the shambles. People always say they live paycheck to paycheck, but we couldn't even live paycheck to two days later. I had talked to Emily about what was going on because she just had to know why I wasn't working there anymore. I told her about the suit. I am dead serious, she called me and said, "I have connections and I happen to know there is no suit." Really, check in hand says otherwise. Found out a few months later that she actually called Allen and asked him. God help me, please let them get divorced. Why me? I stayed on unemployment for a couple months and finally found a job with a company that hires felons. You can google companies that hire people with felonies and it will list about 30 companies. This was a very prominent company and I disclosed that I had a criminal record, and they still hired me. I started training and felt OK every day with not having the shakes or feeling crappy, but let me tell you when 4 o'clock rolled around I couldn't get home

SUCK IT UP CUPCAKE, IT'S JUST WITHDRAWAL

fast enough, and I chugged two beers quicker than you could imagine. After training, we went into transitions where my hours were later in the day. This was interfering with my drinking so I just stopped showing up. I was a no call, no show, and was out of a job. Jared was starting to mistreat me because he is a very monetary person, but we stayed together. We were able to get bills caught up though, for now. Pap had taken very ill and passed away. I got drunk at his funeral so that I didn't have to deal with things. It hit me but it didn't hit me hard because we had grown distant and to be quite honest, excessive alcohol numbs the emotions and the mood stabilizer I was on helped a lot. I was lucky enough not to be there. Life loss #11.

I received a call that Kedrick, my cousin that I was once so very close with, was unresponsive and in ICU. Jared and I along with the kids and my mother, rushed to the hospital. I was flipping out. It was then, when I realized my utter freaking fear of death. Kedrick had coded a few times but reality has not set in at this point, of thinking he could die. I gathered the boys in the chapel and we said the Lord's Prayer thinking that would help.

SUCK IT UP CUPCAKE, IT'S JUST WITHDRAWAL

Heather looked so thin and frail and just completely exhausted. There were so many of our family members there and everyone was just a mess. Adam Jr. and I walked down to the gift shop and a code came out to Kedrick's room again. We rushed upstairs and as we were walking back, Devon, Kedrick's youngest son grabbed me and said, "he's gone, he's not in pain anymore". I grabbed my aunt, Kedrick's mother, and let out a cry like no other. Poor Heather, she had just lost her partner, the love of her life, the father of her children, and her best friend. My heart broke for her. It was time for the funeral and there is no way at this point that I can look at a dead body. It is almost as if I have a small panic attack even thinking about it. The visitations started at noon and went the entire day, so you know what that means, I drank the entire day. It was not cool for me to get in front of all those people and pass out, but it was cool to smell like a brewery. That was my thought process. Everyone could tell I was drunk by the later part of the day and that bothered me a little, but I didn't have to face death so it was a win win for me. I ran into Heather a few weeks later and she was so thin, with a skeleton appearance and I knew she was taking his death so very hard. This is life loss #12.

SUCK IT UP CUPCAKE, IT'S JUST WITHDRAWAL

The company I had just quit working for called me to come back. Hello, I was a no call, no show, for a month. I decided we needed the money and went back to work. This lasted about a month. They switched me to the 5 pm to 1:30 am shift. I refuse to go without seeing my children, plus how am I supposed to drink? I ended up walking off the job after the second night of this. I was unemployed again. I looked everywhere for something and saw a post on Facebook of a neighbor of mine offering to someone else, who was looking for a work from home position, to message her to talk. I messaged her and she responded that I needed to call her. I gave her a call and we talked a little, then she had me call her dad and we talked a lot. I started out going to her house where her husband, Jacob, called dealerships to purchase used cars wholesale, for a new franchise dealership out of Florida. It was a bam bam kind of thing, called then started. At this point my drinking is between the hours of all the time except when at their house and a lot. I started working and I was really good at it. I started in October and by January, started making money, and a lot of it. At this point, when I leave their house to go to my house for lunch, literally a quarter of a mile away, I would guzzle two beers to hold off the shakes. I was hiding the drinking because I didn't want my kids, husband or mother to think I was an alcoholic. At the beginning of January, I started drinking before I would go to work, drinking at lunch, and then drinking when I left. I even once put beer in a mug, and left it in my car while at their house to drink in between. The morning drinking started to become a habit. One morning I woke up at 5 am with the shakes and anxiety. I drove to the gas station that didn't start selling beer until 5:30 am. I waited in my car till then, grabbed a six pack and made up a bull shit story about my husband still in a Texas Hold Em tournament and the guys needed beer. The relief I would feel when I got that first beer down was astonishing. How it changed me from a frazzling, weak Parkinson's victim, to a regularly functioning human being. I drank from sun up to sun down, with a few hours before and after. In my head, I knew I had a serious problem, but had no harmful consequence at this point. I would sneak a beer or two up into my bedroom, drink It down quick, and then throw the beer can under my bed.

My mother was truly getting to me. I drank a lot to not have to deal with the fights she would start every day. It was constant lies and my brother would call me fighting with me about it. Since she was old and I am the ex-con, obviously, I am the liar. She was watching the kids one day and started on Adam Jr., then went on to smack him in the face. I gave her an ultimatum, she goes to mental health, or she gets evicted. She had hit me a few times before this

SUCK IT UP CUPCAKE, IT'S JUST WITHDRAWAL

and it took every ounce of every bit of control I had in me to not drop her right there. She called lying to my brother, again, so my brother called me starting a fight. He told me I killed our dad and went on to just dog me out. Jared overheard him and proceeded to call him leading to a huge fight. I was in shock that Jared stood up for me, but it's OK for him and his family and friends to say what they want to and about me, but no one else can. My mom went to mental health a couple times but because the counselor agreed with me, she said she didn't need it anymore. All I could keep doing was to tell her to get her own place. She was starting to affect the kids even though they love her with all they have. She would constantly call Jared names and told me one day she wished I was never born. I understand that the commandments state that your supposed to honor your parents, but when your parent is destroying you daily and cutting your throat, you dismiss that commandment. Never let anyone, and I mean anyone, destroy you. We had a bunch of people over and my mom went upstairs to get her cat and she seriously came down and told everyone about the beer cans under my bed. She didn't care about anything but herself. My brother is the same way. He's a good dad but everything revolves around him. He has always been jealous of me and complains my mother shows more attention to me and my kids but it really is because we treated her like a

SUCK IT UP CUPCAKE, IT'S JUST WITHDRAWAL

human and he didn't. That is until she went psychotic. I finally had enough of everything and decided to quit drinking. I knew I would feel bad but had no idea of what was soon to follow. Why when we decide to do something good, like stop an addiction, do we suffer so much. Opiate withdrawal sucked but it was livable and just uncomfortable, unlike alcohol, which is just plain scary.

SUCK IT UP CUPCAKE, IT'S JUST WITHDRAWAL

CHAPTER 11-TO PASS OUT, OR NOT TO PASS OUT, THAT IS THE QUESTION

I stopped the drinking on a Tuesday. Wednesday and Thursday, I felt like I had a bad case of the flu and on Thursday I felt like jelly and numb. I woke up Friday morning feeling pretty much OK. I went in the bathroom to get ready to go to work and suddenly everything went black. It was if I passed out, but didn't go all the way out. I had the weirdest feeling come over me. It was as96 if I were warm on the inside, drunk but without the feeling good part, and I mean schmammered, shaking uncontrollably and faint. I came to and thought it was just a spell from stopping drinking, which it was, but it would come and go

SUCK IT UP CUPCAKE, IT'S JUST WITHDRAWAL

the entire day until I had to leave work and come home.
My mom tried to take my blood pressure but as the cup
tightened, I would almost pass out. I begged Jared to take
me to the ER but he refused, he didn't want to take time
out of his day. My mom finally took me and when I arrived
at the hospital, I felt a little better. I advised triage that I
had quit drinking three days earlier but told them I
thought I was having a bad reaction with the antidepressant I started two days earlier and Midol. They
didn't even mention alcohol withdrawal. They took my
blood pressure several times in several different positions
and it was fine. Blood work showed I was low on
potassium and they gave me a horse pill to take. The
doctor told me he was going to give me a shot of Ativan. I
refused, I was sitting there in alcohol withdrawal but used
my Chemical Dependency training as a reason to tell them
no, because of how addictive and bad benzos can be for
you. I left the ER and went home to lie down. Finally, I
took my Ziprasidone and Benadryl and went to sleep but
not before the meds induced another spell. I fell asleep
and woke the next morning feeling crappy but not having
the horrid attacks. I was scared to death one would hit
though. Later in the day, I started feeling back to normal
and breathed a huge sigh of relief that it just might be

over. As the days went on I noticed my nerves were shot. I was also missing the buzz feeling that I had every day before I quit drinking. I started taking a dose of the Ziprasidone and Benadryl during the day and that seemed to help for a while. At this point my chemistry has been changed and my neurons have been completely altered. I drank a few times and really had no problems. I made sure it wasn't on consecutive days and was few and far between. Jared was making comments that I was so overly lovey and happy. Well, hell yeah, I thought I was going to die not too long ago. I was very lucky though, on day three of withdrawal from alcohol, the DT's can kick in. I have seen people in rehab have them and they have no idea where they are, they are delirious. Hallucinations of seeing and hearing things that aren't there. I also avoided a seizure. Those usually occur in the first 10 days after quitting. I started drinking one day at noon. It just didn't feel the same so I decided to stop around 6 pm. I started feeling bad and then went into full blown panic attack mode. I was faint and my heart I thought was in a race. I decided that was it for me, at least for a few years.

I had surgery to remove a pin in my tow that was put there two years earlier to repair a bad break. I was given pain meds and took them for about a month before and after the surgery. I was really enjoying the high from

SUCK IT UP CUPCAKE, IT'S JUST WITHDRAWAL

them but when the doctor offered me more, I said no, because I knew what they would do to my life. After I stopped the pills I went to my family doctor to talk to him about increasing the Ziprasidone to a small day dose as well. He agreed and called in the script. Haley, my first-born granddaughter, had a temper. When she would hold her breath, I stated to black out. The medication helped before when I would take it so I thought I would keep doing the day time dose. The doctor also had given me a prescription for an antidepressant that helps you quit smoking. I waited a few weeks to start that. I was taking it for about a week and had the most horrific episode to this day I can't explain other than a drug interaction. I was standing there in my kitchen, and my entire face went numb, my heart was racing so hard you could see it, and I could not swallow at all. I cringe today thinking about it. It subsided only to happen again a little later. I stopped the antidepressant and then the anxiety kicked in. For two days, from just a month of use, I was having withdrawal from the antidepressant. I drank a little here and there after this but it just didn't feel the same anymore. I had blood work done that showed I had high calcium levels in my blood which is a result of hyperparathyroid disease and I read that alcohol could make it worse. I stopped drinking right then and have never drank again. I also developed hypoglycemia from drinking. Alcohol is the most detrimental drug on the body and if the withdrawal

SUCK IT UP CUPCAKE, IT'S JUST WITHDRAWAL

doesn't kill you, the diseases it causes may. I started taking the Ziprasidone intermittently which was a really bad idea because it is supposed to be taken at the same time every day as to not cause withdrawal. I had been on it for years and had only went without my bedtime dose once, leaving me to not sleep and feel crappy, but that was about it, so I had no idea of the withdrawal, yet. This begins the worst years of my life that I wouldn't wish on my worst enemy. This is life loss #13, this part of my life rocked me to my core and despite all the losses I suffered, my physical health was by far the most devastating and at times made me envy who had passed because they are at peace. At this time, we went down south so that Kendal and Redtick could get married, Kendal was pregnant again. Baby Halena was born in October, and she was a living doll. I almost passed out several times at the hospital but I made it through somehow. Jared and I were fighting pretty bad at this time and I had decided that I wanted a divorce. I had to make him feel bad for him to go see the baby but he did. Somehow, we worked it out again.

SUCK IT UP CUPCAKE, IT'S JUST WITHDRAWAL

CHAPTER 12-WHAT THE WHAT?

I get compliments all the time on how gorgeous the two boys are. I decided to get Adam Jr. into modeling so we drove to Cincinnati for an audition, Landen is just a little too young at this point. They loved him. He had to start going to classes but the drive was well worth it. Landen and I would sit in the break room and wait on him. I was feeling fine all day and then, while we are two hours away from home, the most ungodly feeling came over me. I couldn't breathe, a pins and needles feeling came over my entire body, I was dizzy and just felt so horrific. I didn't know what to do so I took a Ziprasidone. Within 40 minutes, I started feeling better. We made it home and the pill had made me very tired and hungry and when I tried to eat, I could barely swallow. I went to bed and woke to felt fine the next day. A couple days later, I took my regular mile

SUCK IT UP CUPCAKE, IT'S JUST WITHDRAWAL

long walk and came back home to sit in the sun for a while. I was sitting there and started shaking uncontrollably and was starting to feel faint. I walked inside and was sure I was going to pass out so in a panic, I called my doctor. She thought I was having a hypoglycemia attack and advised me to eat something quick. I grabbed bread and shoved it down my throat. I could barely talk because I felt like I was blacking out. A few minutes later it started to pass but I was still shaking and felt like a train hit me. My husband took me to the ER and they found nothing wrong. The next day I scheduled a doctor appointment and was sent for a glucose test. The test showed I was borderline hypoglycemic but that didn't explain the episodes I was having. It was then that it dawned on me that I was taking the Ziprasidone sporadically. I then decided I should take it every morning when I woke up to avoid these problems. I would take it at around 8 am and sleep for a couple hours, or mostly lay down because I couldn't fall asleep, but was exhausted. By 2 pm I would feel anxiety, so I decided to take another pill. This went on for a while and I realized my job was suffering

SUCK IT UP CUPCAKE, IT'S JUST WITHDRAWAL

and I wasn't playing with my kids as much as I usually did. I decided to go off of the medication and knew I had to taper to avoid the really bad withdrawal symptoms I previously had. At this time, we found out that Craig, Jared's amazing dad, had ALS.

I started out by dumping a little bit out of each capsule but this was a really bad idea because the milligrams will be different in every dose. The first drop was ok, I had anxiety for a few days and felt kind of malaise over my body. I stayed at this level for about two weeks. Usually my evenings were much better for some reason, but at this point I am very dopamine sensitive so my symptoms fluctuated day by day. I dropped again, dumping a little more out of the capsules and would measure by the amount left in the capsule. This was getting exhausting. I decided to make one huge drop because the previous two were not killer and I had grown a pair of balls. I dropped one dose all together and halved the other dose. I felt like shit, anxiety riddles, weak and frail, and so shaky. On day four, D-day, I was doing OK and that evening before I was to pick Adam Jr. up from practice, I had a horrific episode. I felt faint like I were going to pass out, my body flushed with warmth, it felt like I had the flu times a thousand, I thought I was dying. Adam Jr.'s coach brought him home after I text and asked him too. The feeling passed and I was so shaky and sick. I took my bedtime dose of the ziprasidone and the horrific feeling went away. I just lost my balls because the next morning I reinstated. Back to 20 mg and 20 mg. I decided to hold this dose through the holidays because I really didn't want to ruin Christmas for anyone, not to mention I love to shop and knew I needed to go out a lot. The holidays passed and I was fairly stable with a few symptoms and always the unbelievable fatigue in the mornings. I was drinking about 10 cups of coffee a day to try and wake up. I was so heartbroken at what a medication could do to me, the same medicine I had taken at bedtime for seven years with no problems at all. I went to see my doctor the first of the year and he explained that we could do a water titration. I researched all I could and found that 20 ml of water is what was needed to mix with 20 mg of the medication. I decided in a week I would start to go down by 10 mg a month and see how that goes, but I get another devastating call.

My brother called and told me they had just found Heather dead in her bed. I lost it. When they found her, she had her hands crossed on her chest. We didn't know if she had a heart attack or what had happened because she was only 41 years old. I was so worried, I had to go to a funeral with a dead body, sober. We went to the funeral and I stayed completely out of the parlor where her body

SUCK IT UP CUPCAKE, IT'S JUST WITHDRAWAL

was lying. I couldn't handle a dead body at this point in my life. All of my family passed me by as I sit with my kids in the entry way. Amber, Heather's sister came to me and we hugged and cried aloud. So many beautiful memories we had together, and now utter heartbreak. My mom wasn't feeling good and she had asked me to drive in the procession. I was sober so I was able to. It was a cold day so when we arrived at the cemetery, I sat in the car with all the kids. I realized that day that I suffered from an irrational fear of death. The thought of it rocked me deep within. I again, went to my doctor and luckily for me he is duel educated in psychology. He gave me my first real diagnosis. OCD, PTSD and thanatophobia, a phobia of death or dying. At least I could finally put a name to all of my problems. I now know that my father's death started a chain reaction within me that would lead me down a path of despair and self-righteousness. I wouldn't allow my children to go in the front yard alone, I constantly had thought of something happening to them that would leave me in tears. I put them in a bubble in hopes to protect them. Could all of the chemicals that have been altering my brain, changes my whole physiology? Heather's death was life loss #14. My mom moved out at this time too and all of the fighting in the house stopped for the most part.

Page 125

SUCK IT UP CUPCAKE, IT'S JUST WITHDRAWAL

It was time to start my taper. I mixed my solution and poured 15 ml of water into my medication spoon and took it. I had dropped my dose down to 30 mg per day. I felt the malaise and anxiety for a couple of days but it was tolerable. I went ahead and went to the doctor because my cough was keeping me up at night and if I don't get a good night sleep, I'm done the next day. I waited a couple of days to take the antibiotics. I went ahead and thought I would try dropping just 2 mg instead of the big 10 mg to see if that would ease the crap feeling I was getting. It was still just as awful. I started the antibiotic without thinking of any effects it may have on me. I was feeling Ok from my drop when on the seventh day, I ended up in the ER. I was shaking and so sick. The ER doctor just figured it was anxiety and wanted to give me a dose of alprazolam. I have always been so scared of benzos but tried it. They gave me .5 mgs to start. Wow, I was goofy out of it. I had to go to the bathroom holding on to walls and when I went to walk out, I ran smack dab into the door. The nurse was walking by at that time and was like, "are you OK?" I told her I felt drunk and she advised me it was the benzo. I felt a little better but very tired and was sent home with a prescription of 20 tablets. I decided the next day that I was going to try and start taking the ziprasidone at bedtime only to see if that would make a difference, and I had the benzo for rescue if it got too bad.

SUCK IT UP CUPCAKE, IT'S JUST WITHDRAWAL

The next day I didn't take my meds. With an anti-psychotic, if you are even an hour late missing your dose time, you have withdrawal, so I felt crappy and shaky. I took an alprazolam and after the usual tiredness that it gives, I felt great, I was able to clean my whole house. I went to get the kids from school and started feeling shaky again so took another one. This made me lethargic and I had to lay down. The next day I was Ok for a while and then took one hoping I could go to the store. It made me very dizzy and sick so I decided not to take them again. The next two days were anxiety riddled. I was on the couch the entire two days. The net day began my lovely fainting episodes that I adore so much. By day six, I couldn't take it and took a 10-mg rescue dose. The next few days were just as if thousands of bees were stinging my nerves and on day 11, I reinstated. By this time, the damage was done and the akathisia set in. For those of you who have experienced this, you know it sucks, for those who haven't, it is a severe bodily restlessness where you have to be moving at all times hoping you can relieve it. You feel like you could jump out of your skin and it is very hard to talk or think. The fatigue was back. I had one day where I felt as if I were going to die. I can't explain it, it was as if my nerves were on fire, the weakness consumed me, I was so dizzy and couldn't sit still. This lasted all morning and finally let up in the evening. Another day, the anxiety had me on my knees and again I had to take

SUCK IT UP CUPCAKE, IT'S JUST WITHDRAWAL

a rescue dose. Finally, after a couple weeks I had gotten stable again and decided to drop 2 mg at a time again and take it very slow. The slower a taper, the less chance of severe withdrawal and relapse, as I have shown you. Getting too eager can be the death of you. I dropped the two milligrams and went through the anxiety until finally I took a Benadryl and it relieved the pain a little bit. The next day I took another Benadryl, and it helped again. Day three of Benadryl, and my body turned to jelly. It was awful. On day three, tolerance kicked in. I was again couch bound. By that night, the Benadryl had worn off and severe anxiety hit me. Could I get shock treatment please? The next morning, I awoke to the same anxiety feeling and said screw it, I took an alprazolam. Oh, my God, the relief I felt was heaven sent. I was able to go spend the day with my daughter and life was good. I called my neurologist, who suggested a benzo at a previous appointment where I declined, and told him it now was a good idea. He gave me a script to take two a day, with five refills, and so begins my benzo ride.

SUCK IT UP CUPCAKE, IT'S JUST WITHDRAWAL

CHAPTER 13-THE GOOD, THE BAD, AND THE BENZO

I started taking the alprazolam with each dose of the ziprasidone. I was goofy for about an hour but was fine after that. This allowed me to drop my ziprasidone by two milligrams, fairly easily. I had one day of a little anxiety but it was very tolerable. I decided to drop weekly. After three weeks, I started having panic attacks. I was very dizzy and again went to the ER. They gave me a vertigo medication and when I got home and took it, I had a chemically induced panic attack. I went to bed and the next day I woke up feeling Ok but noticed about four hours after my dose of alprazolam wore off, anxiety started. I google everything, and googled benzos. I was taking a powerful, short acting benzo. I needed a long acting one. The next week I called my neurologist and made an appointment. I explained to him what was going on so he

SUCK IT UP CUPCAKE, IT'S JUST WITHDRAWAL

switched me to clonazepam and also gave me a prescription of hydroxyzine, which is a powerful antihistamine that calms the central nervous system and helps with anxiety. I asked him if I need to taper off the short acting benzo and slowly introduce the other. He said no but my gut feeling told me he was wrong. I called the pharmacist and asked him, and he advised me I did need to taper in and out. I also googled it over a hundred times cause let's just face it, google is life and when you have OCD, you are the best damn detective in the land. All said to slowly introduce one, while tapering out the other. I took 1 mg of the clonazepam at bed time, and the next day cut my alprazolam in half for each dose. I slowly lowered it over the next few days and went through horrible withdrawal. After a few days if I took the alprazolam, I would get very ill. My nuero advised me that if I needed to still take it here and there, that would be Ok. The lunatic recommended two benzos. I was able to cross over and started my tapering of the ziprasidone again. Two milligrams per month. Nice and slow. We were called to the lake because Jared's father wanted to talk to all of us. He decided he wanted to take his oxygen mask off and pass peacefully with the help of hospice. We supported him because we knew he was suffering. He was such a sweet, giving man, and watching him go was so very hard. I dreamt about it many nights, and I think the peace of it helped me a little. This is life loss #14.

SUCK IT UP CUPCAKE, IT'S JUST WITHDRAWAL

I was finally functioning normally but noticed I was becoming exercise intolerant and rapidly gaining weight. I started back to school, because I had taken time off when I was drinking, it was too much of a burden at the time. I started buying more cars at work and was able to do pretty much anything now. I had a few days when I dropped my dose where I had anxiety, so I thought I would try the hydroxyzine. I cut the huge tablet in half and when I took it, I started panicking because a calm came over my body that was unreal. I was so relaxed but then came with it, fatigue. It made me very tired but that was a small price to pay compared to anxiety. I started using the hydroxyzine regularly and it really was a life saver. I was on the alprazolam for about two and a half months and then the clonazepam for almost five, when I hit the dreaded tolerance withdrawal. I went to the nuero again, where he upped my dose and the day after I was good to go again. I was terrified at this point, with all my schooling I knew that once you hit tolerance, you're going to have withdrawal. I started my googling again and freaked myself out. I wanted off the ziprasidone so bad I was willing to risk it. I dropped my ziprasidone dose again and seemed to be doing pretty good but was suffering from dizziness here and there with the hydroxyzine helping for the most part. At this point my mood is flat. I am constantly yelling at my older son when we had a no yelling policy in our home. Jared and I are drifting further

SUCK IT UP CUPCAKE, IT'S JUST WITHDRAWAL

and further apart because of my constant complaining about symptoms as well as the fact that I had no interest in sex, or even smiling for that matter. I had more anxiety from taking the benzo than I did from withdrawal. I had a big paper due and it was time to get to work on it, I had to force myself to start on it as even little things like bathing are a lot of work at this point. The paper was on the withdrawal effects of stimulants. What the fuck, I'm a depressant girl, time to interview someone. "Jared, where are you?"

Jared did a lot of meth back in California, when he lived there. I started asking him about his usage with how much and how often he used. He explained he smoked it and snorted it every day, until he crashed. He smoked it or snorted it every few hours to keep the effects going and then after four days of being up 24/7, he would sleep for two days, and then start the process all over again. This went on for about a year. He explained to me how he would be so high, he would take electronics apart, just to put them back together again. This is known as Frankensteining. I asked him about the withdrawal. He stated that it started the day after he stopped and lasted for about ten days. He was shaky but yet, so tired, but couldn't sleep. He felt as if things were crawling on his

SUCK IT UP CUPCAKE, IT'S JUST WITHDRAWAL

skin a lot. He speech was slurred and he was a little confused. The least little thing freaked him out. His eyes were red and itchy and he couldn't stop eating. He had lost a lot of weight while he was on it. After his acute was over, he had an unbelievable craving for the drug. I gasped when he explained this to me, relating to some of what he said. It was so weird hearing about a man who is so strong and hard willed, to have suffered in such a way. I asked him, "what made you quit?" He said that his life was becoming unmanageable and he was spending wasted dollars. I think many addicts have said that before. I turned my paper in and received an A on it and thanked Jared for taking the time to help me with it. I thought to myself, Jared and I are so alike, in that we both have been addicts, but we are so different in that he loves stimulants and I love depressants. He also had a bought with cocaine as well.

It was time for me to drop my dose again, and usually it took about 7 to 10 days to start feeling better, but this time was different. I couldn't get stable. You should never lower your dose on a psych drug again, until you have stabilized. I ended up in the ER again because I thought I was having a stroke. I couldn't see out of my right eye and the head pain was unreal along with

SUCK IT UP CUPCAKE, IT'S JUST WITHDRAWAL

dizziness. Was it the clonazepam or the fact that I was getting lower in my dose of ziprasidone. The doctor did a CT scan and it was negative except for a sinus infection, so my nuero doctor called in a nasal spray which helped. I had gotten really tired of the ups and downs with the benzo and decided to check out if our insurance would cover me going to a detox facility. All of the googling of withdrawal from benzos finally got the best of me. I ended up calling a rehab facility in another town to see what my insurance would cover and what I would need to pay. I did an assessment over the phone and they called me the next day to say that my stay would be 100% covered. Jared and I talked about it and he was very supportive. At this time, he was growing as a man. His aggression is almost nonexistent and his temperament is much calmer. We decided to call in my mother and Carol to help with the boys because Jared worked evenings and they needed care. All this time of withdrawal and being so sick, I have taken care of the boys on my own. Yes, I am married, but he is never around. It is as if I am single again. He works over so much because of me not making that much, giving me all the more reason to get off this medication. I set up schedules and had a rock-solid plan with child care and set up the time for me to enter rehab on December 5th, 2016. I was entering rehab, not because I relapsed and was a drug addict again, but because I wanted off of a dangerous drug now, and I didn't want to

SUCK IT UP CUPCAKE, IT'S JUST WITHDRAWAL

have a seizure. If you cold turkey a benzo, you can die.
You have to go to medical detox, or do a very slow taper to
avoid serious problems. I said my goodbyes to my family
as we cried, and I headed out. I called Kendal when I got
there and told her I wouldn't be able to talk to her for a
couple days, and she started balling, this just about killed
me, but I knew I had to get off, I had to stop the process of
being an accidental addict. My mother-in-law has become
a friend now, she let go of any hate and saw that her son
loved me so, and that he had just had issues. I appreciate
her so much and love her like my own mother. I am very
comfortable with leaving the boys with them.

CHAPTER 14-WHY DIDN'T YOU TELL ME IT WAS GOING TO BE THIS BAD

I walked into the rehab facility and was asked to wait in the lobby after I checked in. I sat there for a while and told the receptionist that I had to go to the bathroom really bad. If I don't go when I gotta go, I go, even in my pants. It's happened, have you ever jumped on a trampoline, dribbles. They needed to drug test me so they called for a nurse. About 20 minutes later, she decided to show up. I did the drug screen and she advised me it was negative, uh oh. I asked her if they will still take me and if my insurance would still cover it and she said yes, but it may change the medications that I am given. I was Ok with that and went back into the lobby to wait some more.

SUCK IT UP CUPCAKE, IT'S JUST WITHDRAWAL

When they came to get me, they took me in a room and had me undress for me to be searched. Are you freaking kidding me! We went upstairs and I was taken to a horrid room with nothing in it but a night stand and a bed. I missed home already and knew this was a mistake. That night I did not take my clonazepam, but was given a huge dose of phenobarbital. It was like a bad drunk, I hated it but went to bed. The next morning, I had to get up really early to see the doctor. He laughed at me, when I told him why I was there. He said, "you no addict, why you here." I told him I just wanted off now without having to taper. He put me on an anti-seizure med and a pheno taper schedule for five days. I did really well in detox, only having two short episodes of not feeling the best, that passed quickly. By day five I had gotten in three arguments because the patients there were treated like prison inmates and my counselor was a bitch. I could teach all of the classes we were going to and had more credentials than many of the counselors and TAs. I asked the doctor on day five, since I was done with the pheno taper, if it was safe for me to go home, and she said it was. I left that day with no money at all, no house key, and my cell phone had died. On the drive home, I was zoning. My head felt so weird I can't even describe it. I got home and had to go to the neighbor's house to call Jared to let me in the house. He was shocked to hear that I had left. I couldn't live without

SUCK IT UP CUPCAKE, IT'S JUST WITHDRAWAL

my family anymore. They are my heart and soul. Jared got home and held onto me as tight as he could and was acting like a kid in a candy store. This is the beginning of the hardest battle I have ever fought. I had no idea what was to come.

     My daughter came over with the girls and for the first time in a long while, I felt so much love. The boys were with their dad for the weekend and I had to wait an entire day before I would get to see them. I was just feeling kind of cock eyed and raw. I filed a contempt on the boys' dad because he wouldn't pay child support in December, for the last eight years, and I had enough of it, but he was wanting the boys to go to Florida with him on Christmas break. You can't pay child support but you can afford Florida. I went down to the courts and had to return three different times because I was so confused. My thinking was just stupid. I was on day nine at this time of being off. On the drive home I was starving, and I felt like my head was going to pop off. I ate and I felt better but still like shit. The next day I woke and had to get Jared up to take the boys to school. I had caught a case of the benzo flu. I had horrific chemically induced anxiety, topped off with severe dizziness and feeling faint. I was in

SUCK IT UP CUPCAKE, IT'S JUST WITHDRAWAL

acute withdrawal and day 10 was my peak. I knew it was going too good. I missed my son's Christmas concerts that night because I couldn't even see straight I was in so much agony. At this time, I was taking the hydroxyzine as a sleep aid as well. I took my ziprasidone and hydroxyzine and headed to bed, praying every second that God would make it stop. As I lie in bed, calm started coming over my body and I drifted off into a peaceful sleep. The next day wasn't near as bad and I had my mom cove over to clean my house because I still just felt a lot of malaise. The next couple of weeks were fairly uneventful. I had days where I felt as if I were on an acid trip, and other days' tinnitus and severe head pressure. On New Year's Eve, we went to my mother-in-law's house to watch the football game. I was feeling ugh, but Ok. After that we went to Kendal's house to spend the night with her. Anna and her husband, met us there and we really enjoyed ourselves. Anna brought her famous tequila that Anna and I could always handle, however, Jared and Kendal, could not. I started feeling severe head pressure at around 11 pm or so but worked through it. Jared was smashed. Anna was taking our pictures and it was at this point that It really hit me, that I had gained 37 pounds from being on the benzos. Please, do not post those damn pictures. Also, my hair was short, I had gotten tired of the extensions and took them out. My face was the same, only it looked 10 years older. I was a different person. This brought depression. We ended the night with Jared passing out and falling on his face, but it was good because I was able to get out.

At around 60 days off, I had an episode. I felt like I was going out of my mind. I couldn't breathe, my heart was pounding, I couldn't sit still or lie still at all, and I felt like I needed to go to the ER, or die. I knew they wouldn't do anything for me so I just waited it out. I started my period that day too so I had the cramps. I was wondering if they were related but wasn't sure. Finally, as the afternoon passed, it let up but I was left feeling like crap the rest of the day. A couple of days later, after my period had ended, I had the most beautiful two-day window. I thought I was healed, I thought this nightmare of 24/7 suffering was over. I walked outside for 40 minutes each day, and bought a gym membership. I was on cloud nine. Only for the next day, to bring back all of my symptoms. I finally was able to go to the grocery store, for the first time in almost a year, without the grocery cart holding me up. In my mind, I am still reserved because I have 18 milligrams of ziprasidone to still taper off of, but needed the withdrawal from the benzo to end first. The next day I awoke to being ill again. What the hell is going on. I googled benzo withdrawal relentlessly and read all about the windows and waves of benzo withdrawal. I was

SUCK IT UP CUPCAKE, IT'S JUST WITHDRAWAL

heartbroken again. My symptoms at this point are annoying and I am just ready for them to be done. I have literally been in withdrawal for two years at this point. My body is going to get sick of it and just tell me to fuck off and quit. I awoke one day to the deepest depression. Nothing caused it, no one set me off. I cried all day and had a feeling someone had put me in a casket and put me in the ground. A dark shroud covered me. I yelled at God and asked him why he had done this to me. How could he let this happen? The day passed and the next I awoke in a much better mood. I googled bad karma, and was sure that was the reason. I was paying for my past. I begged God to forgive me and asked how I could make it right.

Month three was by far the worst for me. I hit a two-week wave with 24/7 symptoms. I thought something was really wrong with my brain because my right eye hurt so bad. I couldn't see anything; my vision was so blurry. My left arm just ached and I felt as though something was wrong with my heart. Obviously, this was the month for paranoia. Insomnia also started in this month surprisingly since I was taking a cocktail of an anti-psychotic, and anti-histamine to go to bed. Hydroxyzine really is the best thing that could have happened to me. I went to a cardiologist, a rheumatologist, and any other doctor I could find. They all said they found nothing wrong. I had

SUCK IT UP CUPCAKE, IT'S JUST WITHDRAWAL

another beautiful window that lasted one day, but the next day, I woke up. Benzo withdrawal is not linear. You don't get the gradual improvement in symptoms like you do with other drugs. You can feel good for a week and then like you are dying the next. At this point my stomach is just gone and I also learned at this time of the food sensitivities. I ate Chinese food and ended up with really bad anxiety and a migraine headache, so I completely changed my diet. No MSG, no preservatives, no coffee and when I ate ice cream, I developed severe head pressure, so no sugar. At 100 days out, I was hit with an anxiety state that wouldn't let up for three days, luckily, the hydroxyzine took the anxiety away but I was left dizzy and tired for the day. On day 104, it was as if I had the most severe sinus pressure and dizziness in my head that I ended up in bed all day. On day 105, things let up, but I was a little loopy all day. I had a couple more days of weird symptoms and then a beautiful window on day 109. I cleaned the entire house, worked out, and did a lot of my school work. On day 110, it was time to go to court for the contempt and I started getting sick. It was possible the stress had triggered it but I don't know for sure. Court went well and we agreed on things with no harm done to either party, but rather to my benefit. A huge weight had been lifted. That evening we went to visit my in-laws, and sat and talked all night. The head pressure was   .

unbelievable. I hadn't eaten in a few hours and thought this may be the problem. I ate and the pressure let up. The next day I woke up, and the most beautiful window again. I was starting my period and still feeling good. Not like run a marathon good, but almost symptom free. Going on four months is where it seems I turned a corner. I will have to for a while, eat a very strict diet. The symptoms from cold turkey withdrawal can last for a year, but I am hopeful that that will not be the case. My marriage with Jared is now just a piece of paper. This venture has made us strangers. We don't touch and we pretty much don't even like each other anymore. I see him for who he is now, and not what I want him to be. I am now finishing my last CDC class and have an ambition that I have never had before. I will not reinstate, and I will survive. I am at the point, that I will not put anything in my body again. If I make it off of the remaining dose of ziprasidone that I am on, I will be in 7th heaven. I believe the benzo withdrawal has prepared me to accept withdrawal and not fight it. It is the most horrific of all of the withdrawals to go through, because it lasts so damn long. I had so many withdrawal symptoms that I couldn't begin to list them all, but know it does get better with time, and you will prevail and win the fight. I started now looking for a real job out of the house.

SUCK IT UP CUPCAKE, IT'S JUST WITHDRAWAL

I interviewed a couple times and then had the idea of going into car sales. I have product knowledge and I need money for a complete makeover, paying bills would be good too. I sent resumes and got an email from a dealership in Columbus. I interviewed and got the job. In order to get a sales license to sell cars I have to be fingerprinted for my criminal record. I was completely honest on my app and they were highly aware of my era of being a jailbird but hired me anyway. My start date was set for May 1st, but at two weeks prior to that I started my period and got hit with symptoms again so the worry set in I wouldn't be able to work. I started my job and was feeling much better. When they cut me loose to sell cars two weeks later, I rocked it and was making it rain until that bitch of a period hit me again. The symptoms weren't as bad so I still functioned OK and had a good month five. Finally, some hope. Six months to the day hit and I entered...the sixth month, low life, suck balls, six-month wave. I was in acute all over again. Old symptoms came back, I was dizzy, had anxiety, panic attacks, and felt like I was going to die. I had to leave work early one day I was so sick, but I pushed through. The thought of reinstating even crossed my mind on a day I had horrid depression. I did have a couple normal days in that month that I actually realized that I was still in love with my husband, so we had mad crazy sex and I rode it like a horse. I was very proud of myself. Then the next day, I didn't like him or have

SUCK IT UP CUPCAKE, IT'S JUST WITHDRAWAL

interest in sex with him. The wave lasted an entire month. At the very end of the month, things started letting up. Hope is yet again returning, but in the back of my head, I know, it will come again. I don't feel great at this point but I am functioning and actually was able to go to the lake, and some what enjoy myself. I was also drinking a lot of diet soda in month six, so I stopped that, and maybe that is why it is letting up again, or maybe time really is the only healer. The amazing thing is in my seven months of withdrawal, I haven't ended up in the ER, yet. Before I was going all the time. I now am tired of the withdrawal, but since I have had all day windows where I feel amazing, I know that is what I am heading for, maybe someday. I start with a personal trainer next week and am ready to get my life back. I get sick of seeing people on TV living normal lives, because I dream of that. I have so many regrets in my life, and every single one of them, are due to an addiction. I have God and my family to keep me alive, in good days, and in bad. My symptoms at seven months are now just uncomfortable and really getting on my fucking nerves, but I think they will end, and when they do, I'm gonna party like it's 1999.

SUCK IT UP CUPCAKE, IT'S JUST WITHDRAWAL

CONCLUSION

Bad things happen to good people. Good things happen to bad people. It is the way of the universe. We are born, we live, and we die. The only thing that is promised in this world is death. There are so many options that we can choose as an alternative, to picking up a drug to make us feel better. I have lived with regrets for years on what made me do it. Today I realized that I needed to go through these things so that I may be able to help others in their time of despair. Life is fucking hard, but people have been living it for many years, drug and alcohol free. If you have done the unspeakable, know that Jesus died for our sins. If you do not believe in God, then

SUCK IT UP CUPCAKE, IT'S JUST WITHDRAWAL

getting past those things may be a little easier for you, maybe not. They say time heals all wounds, I say they never heal, we just deal with them differently. If you are going through withdrawal, know it will pass, but with each new addiction, the pain gets worse. Our bodies are temples and should be treated as so. I personally have decided to not put anything that may harm or cause addiction, into my body. We all have the right to choose. Because of the harrows I have gone through, this is my choice. It used to be getting buzzed was a highlight, now it is just feeling normal, that gives me a high. If you feel that all is lost and there is no hope, know that many have gone before you, and many have healed. I have not been charged with a crime, in 10 years, and I am now able to get a good job just about anywhere. I find that it is in my darkest moments, that I see the light. Maybe once I finish my clinicals and start my own practice, I will be seeing you, or maybe you will wise up before then, or maybe you will OD again, time will tell. It is so much better on the sober side of life. If you have children, I pray that you chose to be the best parent you can be. If you love your mother, I pray that you do not put her through anymore despair. If you have a significant other, I pray you stop breaking their heart. I pray you are lucky enough to go through withdrawal, but most of all, I pray that you choose to go through it in the first place. I think I have earned the right to say "don't be a self-centered pussy." I have been lucky

SUCK IT UP CUPCAKE, IT'S JUST WITHDRAWAL

not to have done prison time or died. Will you be as lucky as I have, why take that chance? Do yourself a solid and get your shit together, not just for others, but for yourself. Oh ya, don't google withdrawal, because your gonna read a bunch of stories, about a bunch of people, about a bunch of symptoms, and throw yourself into an anxiety attack. Man up, and take one for the team. Bye Felicia.

Printed in Great Britain
by Amazon

70932774R00086